Well Said

Advanced
English
Pronunciation

Linda Grant
*Georgia Institute
of Technology*

Heinle & Heinle Publishers
A Division of Wadsworth, Inc.
Boston, Massachusetts 02116 U.S.A.

Vice President and Publisher: Stanley J. Galek
Editorial Director: David C. Lee
Developmental Editor: Nancy Mann
Assistant Editor: Kenneth Mattsson
Project Manager: Stacey Sawyer, Sawyer & Williams
Editorial Production Manager: Elizabeth Holthaus
Production Editor: Kristin Thalheimer
Manufacturing Coordinator: Mary Beth Lynch
Text Design: Nancy Benedict
Illustrations: Anne Eldridge and Pat Rogondino
Cover Art: Laura K. Popenoe
Cover Design: Bortman Design Group

Copyright © 1993 by Heinle & Heinle Publishers
All rights reserved. No parts of this publication may be reproduced or transmitted in any
form or by any means, electronic, or mechanical, including photocopy, recording, or any
information storage and retrieval system, without permission in writing from the publisher.

Manufactured in the United States of America

Heinle & Heinle Publishers is a division of Wadsworth, Inc.

Library of Congress Cataloging-in-Publication Data

Williams, Linda Verlee.
        Well said : advanced English pronunciation / Linda Grant.
            p.   cm.
        ISBN 0-8384-3963-2
        1. English language—Pronunciation.   I. Title.
    PE1137.W63   1993
    428.3'4—dc20   92-40903
                                                                                          CIP

ISBN 0-8384-3963-2

10   9   8   7   6   5   4   3   2

Contents

· · · · · · · · ·

Appendices

To the Teacher
. . . .

This textbook is designed to improve the speech intelligibility of high-intermediate to advanced learners of American English as a second language. It was written with the general ESL/EFL population in mind but should be especially useful for learners who wish to communicate more clearly in academic, business, scientific, and professional settings.

Well Said addresses the pronunciation needs of students from a variety of language backgrounds. The body of the text focuses on problems of sound/spelling patterns, syllables, word endings, linking, stress, rhythm, and intonation common to students of most language backgrounds. The appendices provide individualized practice for consonant and vowel problems, which can vary widely in most groups of students.

Because of the learner-centered, interactive nature of many of the practices, Chapters 1 through 10 are intended for classroom use. All but the open-ended exercises, however, are prerecorded for independent use. The segmental practices in the appendices are designed for independent laboratory use but can be used with groups of students in the classroom if the teacher desires.

Special Features of the Text

The pronunciation teacher in today's classroom faces a number of problems. Here are a few:

- Individualizing the pronunciation curriculum to meet the diverse needs of a group of learners

- Guiding learners into natural, relevant speaking contexts so that carryover of pronunciation skills into communication is not left entirely to chance

- Establishing realistic goals and reasonable measures of progress that account for destabilization during learning, different rates of acquisition, and the role of the learner in evaluation and monitoring

- Identifying an integrated pronunciation curriculum that precludes the need for heavy supplement of teacher-made materials or texts from other skill areas

In response to these and other problems, **Well Said** offers the following distinctive features:

- An introductory chapter for identifying individual pronunciation needs and priorities

- A gradual progression from controlled practice into relevant, natural communicative contexts

- An approach that encourages peer monitoring and self-evaluation

- Integration of pronunciation with other skill areas, especially listening and discourse-level speaking formats

- Emphasis on stress, rhythm, and intonation as the features of speech that have the greatest impact on intelligibility

- Special sections in the appendices that provide a comprehensive overview of segmentals and intensive practice with troublesome consonants and vowels

- Activities that maximize student talking time and provide sufficient practice to enable students to assimilate elements of clear speech into oral communication

Organization of the Text

The primary organizational focus is pronunciation. Each pronunciation point is integrated with listening activities, a hierarchy of speaking activities moving from structured to more spontaneous tasks, and linguistic and cultural information to support the suggested communicative activities.

The text has ten chapters and three appendices. Chapter 1 includes an individualized evaluation instrument and tools for learner self-evaluation and goal setting. These instruments yield valuable individual and class profiles, alert the teacher to the parts of the book that need special emphasis, and serve as motivational devices for the students.

Chapter 2 explores the use of the dictionary for pronunciation purposes and simultaneously introduces students to pronunciation points covered more extensively in later chapters.

Chapter 3 clarifies some unusual sound/spelling patterns in English and provides concentrated practice with final consonant sounds. Teachers can refer to the consonant overview (Appendix B) and vowel overview (Appendix C) as needed.

Chapter 4 covers syllables and grammatical endings. Chapters 5 through 10 address the stress, rhythm, and intonational features of American English.

A standard format is used in Chapters 3 through 10. Each chapter begins with a section called *Listen,* designed to enhance aural awareness of the target pronunciation feature in each chapter and to build skills for peer and self-monitoring.

In the next section, *Rules and Practices,* students are encouraged to discover pronunciation **Rules** and regularities. Structured and semi-structured **Practices** help students gain control of the pronunciation features before applying the skills in the communicative contexts.

In the *Communicative Practice* sections of Chapter 4 through 10, learners incorporate pronunciation concepts into contextualized speaking activities that elicit, as naturally as possible, many instances of the feature under study. These activities guide learners as they bridge the gap between a focus on the accuracy of a pronunciation feature to a focus on meaning.

Following communicative activities, most chapters have a special section called *Extend Your Skills* that recycles the target pronunciation skill into discourse-level speaking formats (i.e., explaining a graph, solving a problem, participating in a discussion, completing a contrastive analysis, and describing a process). This section also includes suggestions for audiotaping, videotaping, and self-evaluation.

Most chapters end with a short *Oral Review,* which students can complete on audiocassette, in an individual consultation, or with a small group. Incentives and strategies for pronunciation practice appear under the headings *Something to Think About* and *A Helpful Hint.* In addition, activities that help students prepare for the Test of Spoken English (TSE) or the SPEAK Test are designated throughout the text.

Appendix A (*Beyond the Pronunciation Class*) contains suggestions for retaining and strengthening pronunciation skills acquired during the class. Appendix B (*Consonants*) and Appendix C (*Vowels*) contain an overview of all consonants and vowels, as well as intensive practice with problematic segmentals. In Appendices B and C, each segment has *Listen* and *Practice* exercises for individual use, as well as *Communicative Practice* for in-class reviews or out-of-class group assignments. The Answer Keys for Appendices B and C are at the end of the text.

The vocabulary in the lessons is challenging and pertinent to various academic and work settings. Discussion of vocabulary can be a valuable part of each lesson. Students have opportunities throughout the text to personalize vocabulary and to practice terminology specific to their fields of work or study.

Teachers are advised to progress through most chapters in sequence. Suggestions for reordering chapters are included in the *Teacher's Manual.* Spiraling throughout the chapters provides the students the opportunity to review previously learned material while integrating new skills. Decisions about deleting or extending speaking activities can be based on the needs and interests of the class, whether it be a quarter-, semester-, or workshop-length course.

Finally, the format of the text enables the instructor to function as a guide or facilitator and encourages the learner to be an active, involved participant in the process of becoming a clear speaker.

Supplementary Materials

Well Said is accompanied by a *Teacher's Manual* and audio program. The manual contains an Answer Key and transcripts for Chapters

1 through 10, as well as teaching suggestions, additional exercises, theoretical information, and a complete list of references. The audio program enables students to work through the text independently and to obtain additional out-of-class practice. Teachers can use it in the classroom at their discretion.

Progress in Pronunciation Improvement

Although there is a clear need for more research into pronunciation learning in a second or foreign language, here are some characteristics of pronunciation development that you may notice among learners of English.

1. There will be individual variation in the rate and extent of pronunciation improvement. Improvement may be influenced by such factors as motivation, aptitude, personality, nature of the first language, language learning strategies, and amount of English spoken outside of class.

2. New pronunciation skills are acquired over time. In the beginning stages, use of a new skill will require conscious attention. Over time and with practice, the skills may become more automatic. New skills often manifest themselves in controlled speaking or reading activities before they are apparent in spontaneous speech. New skills may be most difficult to incorporate when the communication and cognitive demands on the learner are heavy.

3. Errors are an expected and natural part of the learning process. Learners might approximate features or patterns before they can produce them clearly. While learning new features or rules, learners may overgeneralize them before refining them. They may lose former skills while acquiring new ones. In short, incorrect productions sometimes indicate that learning is occurring.

4. Learners might only partially integrate new pronunciation features into spontaneous speech. However, even partial integration of a new pronunciation skill has a positive overall effect on intelligibility.

I hope that this textbook provides learners with an opportunity to build and enhance pronunciation skills in authentic communication as our knowledge of pronunciation development in a second language continues to grow in the years ahead.

To the Student

. . . .

One of the most difficult aspects of learning another language is mastering the pronunciation. Many of you can read, write, and understand American English well, but you may face situations in which your pronunciation interferes with clear and effective communication. This textbook/audiocassette program is designed to help you improve your pronunciation so that you can communicate confidently and be understood with relative ease.

In this course, you will focus on those pronunciation issues that are common problems for intermediate to advanced learners of English. Practices range from structured exercises to real-life communication activities. The arrangement of activities gives you an opportunity to gain control of new pronunciation skills before practicing them in the types of situations you might encounter in everyday life at work or school. As you progress through the activities in each chapter, your pronunciation of new patterns will gradually require less conscious attention and become more automatic.

Throughout the course you will work individually, in pairs, in small groups, and as a class. You will have many chances to engage in the roles of both speaker and monitor (or listener). As a monitor, you will develop the ability to hear the differences between clear and unclear pronunciation forms in the speech of your classmates. You will also strengthen the all-important ability to monitor and correct your own pronunciation.

Here are a few more points to consider as you begin this course in pronunciation improvement:

- Mistakes are a natural, necessary part of the process of improving pronunciation skills, so don't be afraid of them.

- You probably won't eliminate your accent or speak with 100 percent accuracy. Your goal is to change those aspects of your pronunciation that interfere with your ability to be understood clearly. You do not need to sound like a native speaker of American English to be fully and easily understood.

- Your attitude is an important element in pronunciation improvement. You will make more progress if you are strongly motivated to improve.

- You will make more progress in pronunciation improvement if you practice your English outside the classroom in real speaking situations.

    I hope **Well Said** helps you in your efforts to become a clear speaker of American English and that you enjoy using it as well.

ACKNOWLEDGMENTS

I am grateful to the scholars and teachers who have influenced my thinking about speech, language, and learning over the years: Judy Gilbert, Laura and Richard Kretschmer, Joan Morley, and Rebecca Oxford.

These people deserve special thanks: my colleagues, Karen Tucker Al-Batal and C. A. Johnston, for field testing portions of the book and providing valuable feedback; the following Heinle & Heinle reviewers for their many useful insights and suggestions: Beverly Beisbier (University of Southern California), Kathleen Flynn (Glendale College), Melinda Kodimer (UCLA), Lois Lanier (University of Maryland), Scott Stevens (University of Delaware), Ramon Valenzuela (Harvard University); Nancy Mann of Heinle & Heinle for her adept editorial guidance; my family, especially my husband Jim, for encouragement; and, finally, my students for demonstrating over the years that the combination of motivated learners and effective teaching and learning strategies can make a difference.

Your Pronunciation Profile

A pronunciation profile is a general description of your pronunciation abilities and needs. It is *not* a test. The purpose of a profile is to alert you and your teacher to the parts of this book that will be of most help to you and to the class.

The speaking activities in the first part of this chapter form the basis of your profile. The activities are ordered from easy to more difficult and from structured to more spontaneous.

The pronunciation profile has three parts:

Part A: Paragraph Reading

Part B: Short Responses to Interview Questions

Part C: Peer Introductions

Do as many or as few of the activities as you have time for. The more speaking you do, however, the more accurately your teacher will be able to evaluate your pronunciation strengths and weaknesses.

During all the speaking activities in this chapter, your teacher can use the *Speech Profile Summary Form* on page 11 to record observations. At the end of the course, you might want to repeat Part A, Paragraph Reading, to measure improvement.

The Speech Profile

Part A: Paragraph Reading

Choose **one** of the following three paragraphs and read it as naturally as possible. You can (1) record the paragraph and submit the cassette to your teacher, or (2) read the paragraph in an individual consultation with your teacher. Give your teacher a copy of the paragraph you choose to read.

Reading 1

Have you ever watched young children practice the sounds of the language they are learning? They imitate, repeat, and sing consonant and vowel combinations without effort. For young children, learning to speak a language is natural and automatic. No one would suspect that complex learning is occurring. For adult learners, however, pronunciation of a new language is **not** automatic. It presents an unusual challenge. Why is pronunciation progress in adults more limited? Some researchers say that there are biological or physical reasons. Others say that there are social or cultural reasons. Although there are many unanswered questions, it is important to realize two things about clear speaking. First, pronunciation improvement might be difficult, but it **is** possible. Second, adults can learn to communicate clearly in English without losing their accents or their identification with their native cultures.

Reading 2*

Have you observed the ways people from different cultures use silence? Have you noticed that some people interrupt conversations more than other people? All cultures do not have the same rules governing these areas of communication. Many Americans interpret silence in conversations to mean disapproval, disagreement, or unsuccessful communication. They often try to fill silence by saying something even if they have nothing to say! On the other hand, Americans don't appreciate a person who dominates a conversation. Knowing when to take turns in a conversation in another language can sometimes cause difficulty. Should you wait until someone has finished a sentence before contributing to a discussion, or can you break into the middle of someone's sentence? Interrupting someone who is speaking is considered rude in the United States. Even children are taught explicitly not to interrupt.

*From Deena R. Levine and Mara B. Adelman, *Beyond Language: Intercultural Communication for English as a Second Language* (Englewood Cliffs, N.J.: Prentice-Hall, 1982), p. 23. Reprinted with permission.

Reading 3*

Edward T. Hall is a famous anthropologist who thinks that different cultures have different outlooks on time, space, and personal relationships. He classifies cultures along a continuum according to whether they are high context or low context. In a high-context culture, the circumstances surrounding the message are more important than the message itself. In a low-context culture, the words themselves are important. For example, if an individual negotiates a business agreement in a high-context culture, the reputation of the family is considered. There is little paperwork because verbal promises are trusted. What happens in a low-context culture? Social and family connections aren't always regarded. An agreement generates a lot of legal paperwork because the contract itself is the most important part of the agreement. Can you think of other examples of how individuals might miscommunicate because of differences in cultural attitudes?

*Information adapted from Elizabeth Hall, "How Cultures Collide," *Psychology Today,* July 1976, 66–74.

Part B: Short Responses to Interview Questions

Record brief responses to the following questions of your choice or schedule an individual meeting with your teacher. Speak as naturally as possible for about two minutes.

1. What is your educational background and/or your work history?

2. What is your purpose for studying English?

3. How much English do you speak each day?

4. In what kinds of situations do you speak English?

5. What do you hope to achieve in this class?

Part C: Peer Introductions

In class, work in pairs with a person whom you do not know well. Spend a few minutes interviewing and getting to know your partner. Take brief notes. Use your notes to introduce your partner to the class.

Speech Profile Summary Form

Name _____

The speaking activities in this chapter indicate that you need to concentrate on the following pronunciation points.

Elements of Speech	Difficulties	Examples
CONSONANTS (Chapter 3; Appendix B)		
VOWELS (Appendix C)		
SYLLABLES AND GRAMMATICAL WORD ENDINGS (Chapter 4)		
STRESS IN WORDS (Chapters 5 and 6)		
RHYTHM IN SENTENCES (Chapter 7)		
SENTENCE FOCUS AND SPECIAL EMPHASIS (Chapter 8)		
INTONATION/ PITCH PATTERNS (Chapters 8 and 9)		
THOUGHT GROUPS AND BLENDING (Chapter 10)		

GENERAL DELIVERY (rate of speech, loudness, eye contact, posture, movement, and gestures):

THREE PRONUNCIATION STRENGTHS:

1.

2.

3.

THREE PRONUNCIATION PRIORITIES (elements most in need of practice):

1.

2.

3.

A Needs Assessment

The needs assessment is a tool to encourage you to think about your speaking needs and abilities and to help your teacher design a course to meet those needs.

Read each item and answer **both** A and B. After you complete the items, arrange yourselves in groups of four or five students. Tabulate the results in your group and report the results to the teacher. Report any discussion about why group members answered as they did.

	A. How **important** is this skill to you in your work/studies? (1 = not at all . . . 4 = very)	B. What is your **ability** in this area? (1 = poor . . . 4 = good)
1. Participating in informal conversations	1 2 3 4	1 2 3 4
2. Participating in discussions	1 2 3 4	1 2 3 4
3. Managing group discussions	1 2 3 4	1 2 3 4
4. Giving short presentations	1 2 3 4	1 2 3 4
5. Giving long presentations	1 2 3 4	1 2 3 4
6. Giving information or instructions	1 2 3 4	1 2 3 4
7. Speaking confidently	1 2 3 4	1 2 3 4
8. Speaking clearly	1 2 3 4	1 2 3 4
9. Appropriate stress patterns in words	1 2 3 4	1 2 3 4
10. Appropriate rhythm patterns in sentences	1 2 3 4	1 2 3 4
11. Speaking at a good speed	1 2 3 4	1 2 3 4
12. Appropriate nonverbal communication (eye contact, gestures, etc.)	1 2 3 4	1 2 3 4

What is your easiest speaking situation?

What is your most difficult speaking situation?

In what area above would you most like to improve?

Keep these results. Refer to them throughout the course in order to reassess your abilities and needs.

Setting Personal Goals

How intelligible or capable of being understood are you? How intelligible do you need or want to be? Use the following *Pronunciation Proficiency Continuum* to judge your own intelligibility. First, put a check (√) at a point along the continuum to indicate your intelligibility or pronunciation proficiency **now**. Then put a star (☆) at a point along the continuum to indicate your pronunciation proficiency **goal**.

When setting goals for yourself, be realistic. For most adult students of American English, achieving near-native pronunciation (position 6+ on the continuum) may not be realistic for the following reasons:

It may not be desirable. Your accent is important because it identifies you with your native language and culture.

It may not be necessary. You can speak American English and be fully understood, yet still retain aspects of your accent.

It may not be possible. Most adult learners have great difficulty eliminating all traces of accent.

Pronunciation Proficiency Continuum

```
1            2            3            4            5            6
L_____|_____|_____|_____|_____J
```

1   Has minimal pronunciation proficiency; listener understands only occasional words

2   Is very difficult for listener to understand, even one accustomed to conversing with non-native speakers; constant repetition needed

3   Is somewhat intelligible to native speakers who are accustomed to conversing with non-native speakers; frequent pronunciation variations distract the listener and also prevent understanding

4   Is intelligible to most native speakers; accent and pronunciation variations are somewhat distracting to the listener but usually do not prevent understanding

5   Has obvious accent and pronunciation variations, but these do not interfere with understanding and rarely distract the listener

6   Has barely detectable accent; pronunciation is almost like that of native speaker; rare, isolated mispronunciations, but no evident patterns of error

Keep the results of this proficiency continuum. Refer back to the scale midway through the course to reassess your goals.

The scale on the previous page was adapted from (1) American Council on the Teaching of Foreign Languages (ACTFL), *Proficiency Guidelines* (Hastings-on-Hudson, N.Y.: ACTFL, 1986), by permission of ACTFL. See below for a complete list of references; and from (2) Joan Morley, "EFL/ESL Intelligibility Index," *"How Many Languages Do You Speak?"* Nagoya Gakuin Daigaku: Gaikokugo Kyoiku Kiyo No. 19, Jan./ Feb. 1988.

ACTFL* REFERENCES

American Council on the Teaching of Foreign Languages. *Proficiency Guidelines*. Hastings-on-Hudson, N.Y.: ACTFL, 1986.

Draper, Jamie B. *State Initiatives and Activities in Foreign Languages and International Studies*. Monograph. Washington, D.C.: Joint National Committee for Languages, 1986.

————. *The State of the States: State Initiatives in Foreign Languages and International Studies*. Monograph. Washington, D.C.: Joint National Committee for Languages, 1989.

Eddy, Peter A. "The Effect of Foreign Language Study in High School on Verbal Ability as Measured by the Scholastic Aptitude Test-Verbal." Washington, D.C.: Center for Applied Linguistics, 1981. (ERIC ED 196 312.)

Masciantonio, Rudolph. "Tangible Benefits of the Study of Latin: A Review of Research." *Foreign Language Annals* 10 (1977): 376–377.

National Council of State Supervisors of Foreign Languages. *Distance Learning in Foreign Languages: A Position Paper with Guidelines*. Monograph. National Council of State Supervisors of Foreign Languages, 1990.

New York State Board of Regents. *New York State Board of Regents Action Plan to Improve Elementary and Secondary Education Results*. Albany, N.Y.: University of the State of New York, State Education Department, 1984.

Panetta, Leon. "The Quiet Crisis of Global Competence." Northeast Conference *Newsletter* 30 (Fall 1991): 14–17.

*ACTFL = American Council on the Teaching of Foreign Languages

Using a **D**ictionary for **P**ronunciation

"Hello, I'm Clifton (klĭf'tun) Latimer (lat'ĭ·mēr)."

Introduction to Dictionary Symbols

An American English dictionary can be a useful pronunciation resource, especially when you can anticipate the vocabulary needed for a discussion, class, meeting, or presentation. Dictionaries use special symbols to show pronunciation. These symbols vary from dictionary to dictionary. For example, the *Longman Dictionary of American English*[†] uses a version of the International Phonetic Alphabet (IPA). Other American English dictionaries use a special set of symbols listed in a pronunciation key or pronunciation table in the introduction and at the bottom of each page of most dictionaries.

In this chapter, you will learn about *your* dictionary and the symbols it uses for the following pronunciation features:

1. SYLLABLES: Every vowel sound in a word creates a beat or syllable. Dictionaries separate syllables with a space, a dot (•), or a hyphen (-).

   Note: The syllable breaks for writing are usually indicated in the first entry word and may not match the syllable breaks for pronunciation, which are often indicated in parentheses or between slant lines (/).

Write the number of syllables or beats in these words, according to your dictionary.

Say the words with your teacher or the speaker on the tape.

business   _____

specific   _____

courier   _____

learned, v.   _____

learned, adj.   _____

fatigue   _____

family   _____

When dictionaries show more than one pronunciation in parentheses, the first is the most common form.

2. STRESS: Dictionaries usually indicate the primary stress, the strongest syllable in a word, with a boldface mark (') above, in front of, or behind the stressed syllable. Secondary stress is usually indicated with a lighter mark (') or a lower mark (ˌ). For pronunciation purposes, pay attention to the primary stresses.

Mark the primary or main stress in each of the following words, according to your dictionary.

Say the words with your teacher or the speaker on the tape.

dem	on	strate		hy	poth	e	sis
tech	nol	o	gy	con	duct,	n.	
tech	no	log	i cal	con	duct,	v.	
teen	ag	er		pa	ram	e	ter

Where does *your* dictionary place the mark for primary stress? _____

3. LONG VOWELS: Dictionaries show long vowels with phonetic symbols or vowel letters with macrons (¯). When a vowel has a macron above it, it is pronounced like the letter name.

ā   ē   ī   ō   ū*

Write the vowel symbol your dictionary uses for the italicized vowels in these words. Then find the key word for each symbol in the pronunciation key.

Repeat the words after your teacher or the speaker on the tape.

	SYMBOL	KEY WORD
f**a**c**e** and f**ai**l	_____	_____
gr**ea**se and m**ee**t	_____	_____
aisle and m**igh**t	_____	_____
r**o**le and g**oa**l	_____	_____
use and f**ue**l	_____	_____

4. SHORT VOWELS: Dictionaries show short vowels with (1) phonetic symbols, (2) vowel letters with breves (˘), or (3) vowel letters with no marks above them.

Write the symbol your dictionary uses for the italicized vowels in these words. Then find the key word for the each symbol in the pronunciation key.

Repeat the words after the teacher or the speaker on the tape.

	SYMBOL	KEY WORD
ad and m**a**gazine	_____	_____
y**e**s and exp**e**nse	_____	_____
it and b**ui**lding	_____	_____
h**o**t and c**o**py	_____	_____
l**u**ck and an**o**ther	_____	_____

5. THE SCHWA: The most common vowel sound in American English is the schwa /ə/ as in *a*bout. The schwa is often used for vowel sounds in unstressed syllables.

Example: available = /ə•'ve^{y}l• ə• bəl/

Look up the following words in your dictionary and underline the vowels pronounced as a schwa /ə/.

*u is sometimes designated (yoo) in pronunciation keys

Repeat the words after your teacher or the speaker on the tape.

meth od	com plain
me thod i cal	ac a dem ic
com mon	pro duc tion

6. CONSONANT SOUNDS: Write the symbol your dictionary uses for the italicized letters in each set of words. Then find the key word for each symbol in the pronunciation key.

Repeat the words after your teacher or the speaker on the tape.

	SYMBOL	KEY WORD
zero ra**z**or lo**s**e clo**s**e (verb)	_____	_____
show ti**ss**ue ini**t**ial spe**c**ial	_____	_____
check na**t**ural fu**t**ure si**t**uation	_____	_____
divi**s**ion A**s**ian u**s**ual bei**g**e	_____	_____
joke a**g**ent gra**d**uate sche**d**ule	_____	_____
ma**x**imum e**x**plain e**x**treme a**cc**ept	_____	_____

EXERCISE 1   PART A: Think about key technical or professional vocabulary that you use frequently at school or at work. Write the words below. Put a circle around the words with pronunciations you are unsure of. Look up the circled words in your dictionary and write the pronunciation symbols for each word in the Dictionary Pronunciation column. Say each word once, then twice in a row, then three times in a row, and then four times in a row in slow motion.

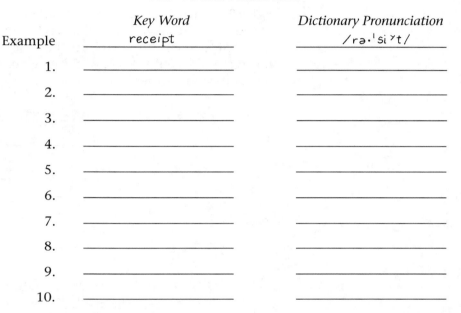

KEY VOCABULARY LIST

	Key Word	*Dictionary Pronunciation*
Example	receipt	/rə·ˈsi ʸt/
1.		
2.		
3.		
4.		
5.		
6.		
7.		
8.		
9.		
10.		

PART B: Create a class list of hard-to-pronounce words by contributing one or two of the most difficult words from each of your lists.

EXERCISE 2   PART A: Think about an upcoming class, meeting, presentation, conversation, or discussion that you will take part in. In the spaces below, write five words that you expect to use and want to pronounce clearly. Write the dictionary pronunciations.

Example 1: Liliana is a graduate student in civil engineering. She looked at her notes for an upcoming class discussion and these are some of the words she wrote down: matrix, reliability, prefabricate.

Example 2: Mehmet is a full-time English student. He could not think of an upcoming situation, so he wrote down some words he had trouble with during his last visit to the infirmary: cough, headache, contagious.

	Your Words	*Dictionary Pronunciation*
1.	_____	_____
2.	_____	_____
3.	_____	_____
4.	_____	_____
5.	_____	_____

PART B: Write a typical phrase or sentence in which you might use each of the five words above. Then say each sentence three times as naturally as possible. Look up from your book as you say the sentences, and imagine that you are really speaking to someone. Dictate your sentences to your partner.

Example: (contagious)   Is the virus contagious? _____

1. _____

2. _____

3. _____

4. _____

5. _____

A HELPFUL HINT

You can improve your overall intelligibility in a discussion or presentation if you correct the pronunciation of just one or two key terms, especially if the terms occur over and over again. Develop the habit of anticipating and checking the pronunciation of key vocabulary you will need for meetings, presentations, and discussions. Look up the words in your dictionary or ask native speakers to pronounce the words for you. You will hear pronunciations that are more natural if you ask native speakers to use the key terms in sentences. Ask native speakers to say the key terms and sentences into a recorder for you. Practice the words and sentences with the native speaker on tape.

Pronunciation Key for *Well Said*

The pronunciation symbols in this text are the same as those used in the *Longman Dictionary of American English.* Some of the symbols look like letters of the alphabet; some do not. Each symbol is printed between slant lines (/) next to a key word to help you pronounce the sound. Complete the chart by writing the symbol your dictionary uses for each sound.

CONSONANTS

Key Word	Symbols	
	Well Said	*Your Dictionary*
1. **p**ie	/p/	
2. **b**uy	/b/	
3. **t**ime	/t/	
4. **d**ime	/d/	
5. **k**ey	/k/	
6. **g**o	/g/	
7. **f**an	/f/	
8. **v**an	/v/	
9. **th**ink	/θ/	
10. **th**em	/ð/	
11. **s**o	/s/	
12. **z**oo	/z/	
13. **sh**oe	/ʃ/	
14. u**s**ual	/ʒ/	
15. **ch**oose	/tʃ/	
16. **j**uice	/dʒ/	
17. **m**y	/m/	
18. **n**o	/n/	
19. ri**ng**	/ŋ/	
20. **l**ed	/l/	
21. **r**ed	/r/	
22. **w**e	/w/	
23. **y**ou	/y/	
24. **h**ow	/h/	

VOWELS

Key Word	Symbols	
	Well Said	*Your Dictionary*
1. h*e*	/iʸ/	
2. h*i*t	/ɪ/	
3. m*ay*	/eʸ/	
4. m*e*t	/ɛ/	
5. m*a*d	/æ/	
6. b*ir*d	/ɝ/	
7. n*u*t	/ʌ/	
*a*bout	/ə/	
8. n*o*t	/ɑ/	
9. t*oo*	/uʷ/	
10. t*oo*k	/ʊ/	
11. n*o*	/oʷ/	
12. l*aw*	/ɔ/	
13. t*ie*	/aɪ/	
14. *ou*t	/aʊ/	
15. t*oy*	/ɔɪ/	

The cartoon at the beginning of this chapter shows dictionary pronunciation symbols for the name **Clifton Latimer.** Write your first and last name below. Using phonetic symbols from this text, write the pronunciation of your name between the slant lines. Ask your partner to pronounce your name using the symbols you wrote.

First Name: _____ /   /

Last Name: _____ /   /

Are there any sounds in your name that do not exist in American English?

3 Sound/Spelling Patterns

"I believe you're right, Professor. It is 'cat' before 'fish,' except after 'bird'."

Drawing by Ralph L. Zamorano. Reprinted by permission of the artist.

One of the most confusing aspects of English pronunciation is spelling. Because English has been influenced by so many other languages, sound/spelling correspondences are irregular. For example, notice how many different ways the letter *g* is pronounced in these words:

get	=	/g/ as in **g**o
a**g**ent	=	/dʒ/ as in **j**uice
bei**g**e	=	/ʒ/ as in u**s**ual

In the following words, notice how many different spellings produce the same /ʃ/ sound as in *sh*oe:

share	=	/ʃ/
ra**t**io	=	/ʃ/
so**c**ial	=	/ʃ/
a**ss**ure	=	/ʃ/
sugar	=	/ʃ/
ma**ch**ine	=	/ʃ/

Some pronunciation problems are related to difficulties in recognizing sound/spelling patterns. This chapter will clarify some consonant sounds and spellings that are especially troublesome. For an overview of **all** the consonants and vowels of American English and for practice with specific sounds, see Appendix B (consonants) and Appendix C (vowels).

Listen!

Listen to your teacher or the speaker on tape present a short passage about the government of the United States. The first time, close your books and listen for meaning. The second time, focus your attention on the sound of each italicized spelling below.

American Government

Many interna**ti**onal students are confused about the government of the United States. They wonder who holds the power and who makes the deci**si**ons. Is the power si**tu**ated in the presiden**ti**al office or in the congre**ssi**onal offices?

The answers go back over two cen**tu**ries. Ever since the days of the American revolu**ti**on, Americans have been suspi**ci**ous of government power. The early Americans believed that England had abused its power and restricted indivi**du**al freedoms. They also believed that the primary role of a na**ti**onal government should be to protect indivi**du**al freedom and to promote self-suffi**ci**ency.

Because of this suspi**ci**on of strong central governments, the writers of the Constitu**ti**on divided power among three branches of the government: the executive (the president), the legislative (the Congress), and the judi**ci**al branches. Although this divi**si**on may not be the most effi**ci**ent way to run a government, it prevents any one branch from obtaining too much power.

Figure 3-2
Organization chart of the United States government.

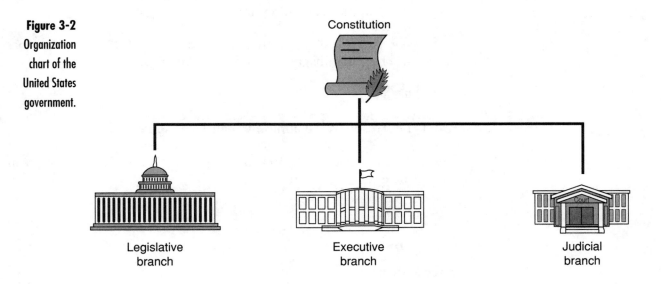

Constitution

Legislative branch

Executive branch

Judicial branch

Several different sounds and spellings were represented in the passage. Did you notice any patterns? In the next section, you will discover the pronunciation rules for the italicized spelling patterns.

Rules and Practices 1: Unusual Consonant Spelling Patterns

The spelling patterns that follow occur in business, academic, medical, scientific, technical, and professional terms. Like most rules of English, these spelling patterns will be true **most** of the time, not **all** of the time.

Rule 3-1

The /ʃ/ sound is commonly spelled *sh* as in *sh*oe.

Listen to the italicized letters in the phrases below. Which sound do you hear in each column? Circle it.

/t/ or /ʃ/?	/s/ or /ʃ/?	/s/ or /ʃ/?
-ti-	**-ci-**	**-ssi-, -ssu-**
the na*ti*onal debt	a so*ci*al event	I a**ssu**re you
essen*ti*al details	a spe*ci*al project	blood pre**ssu**re
presiden*ti*al debate	an effi*ci*ent way	i**ssu**es of today
a ra*ti*o of 7:1	suspi*ci*ous person	severe rece**ssi**on

COMPLETE THE RULE: The *-ti-*, *-ci-*, *-ssi-*, and *-ssu-* in suffixes or word endings are additional spellings for the /   / sound as in _____.

Note: The *ch* spelling in these words also sounds like /ʃ/ as in *sh*oe: machine, chef, champagne, Chicago, and Michigan.

Rule 3-2

The /tʃ/ sound is commonly spelled *ch* as in *ch*oose.

Listen to the italicized letters in the phrases. Which sound do you hear? Circle it.

/t/ or /tʃ/?

-tu-

a tense si*tu*ation

in the near fu*tu*re

na*tu*ral ingredients

the next cen*tu*ry

✔ COMPLETE THE RULE: The -tu- in suffixes and word endings is another spelling for the /   / sound as in _____.

Rule 3-3

The /ʒ/ as in u*s*ual never occurs at the beginnings of words.

Listen to the italicized letters. Circle the sound that you hear in each column.

/z/, /ʃ/, or /ʒ/?	/z/, /ʃ/, or /ʒ/?
-si-	*-su-*
a head-on colli*si*on	a precise mea*su*rement
a minor revi*si*on	expo*su*re to the sun
divi*si*on of power	lei*su*re-time activities
central A*si*a	a ca*su*al acquaintance

✔ COMPLETE THE RULE: The -si- and -su- in suffixes are the most common spellings for the /   / sound as in _____. (Pronunciation Hint: The /ʒ/ = /ʃ/ + *voicing**.)

Rule 3-4

The /dʒ/ sound is commonly spelled *j* (*j*uice) and *g* (*g*enerous).

Listen to the italicized letters. Which sound do you hear?

/d/ or /dʒ/?

-du-

indivi*du*al rights

an e*du*cated guess

a recent gra*du*ate

new proce*du*res

✔ COMPLETE THE RULE: The -du- in the middle of words is another spelling for the /   / sound as in _____.

Find the words in the lists above that you use frequently. Say them silently. Can you think of any other words that are examples of these spelling patterns?

*voicing = vocal cord vibration

EXERCISE 1   With a partner, write the phrases in the correct columns below.

nego**ti**ate a contract ∫	a mu**tu**al friend ₂
very profe**ssi**onal ∫	long divi**si**on ₃
my plea**su**re ₃	resche**du**le the meeting ₄
ra**ci**al balance ∫	your depar**tu**re time ₂
your signa**tu**re ₂	gra**du**al improvement ₄
poor vi**si**on ₃	resi**du**al amount ₄

Column 1	Column 2	Column 3	Column 4
/ʃ/	/tʃ/	/ʒ/	/dʒ/
as in **sh**oe	as in **ch**oose	as in u**s**ual	as in **j**uice
_____	_____	_____	_____
_____	_____	_____	_____
_____	_____	_____	_____

Repeat each list of phrases after your teacher or the speaker on tape.

EXERCISE 2   Add suffixes to the base words and write the new words. Change spellings if necessary.

1. _____   promote + ion =   _____
2. _____   confuse + ion =   _____
3. _____   revise + ion =   _____
4. _____   supervise + ion =   _____
5. _____   grade + ual =   _____
6. _____   decide + ion =   _____
7. _____   literate + ure =   _____
8. _____   divide + ion =   _____
9. _____   please + ure =   _____
10. _____   event + ually =   _____
11. _____   close + ure =   _____
12. _____   conclude + ion =   _____
13. _____   discuss + ion =   _____
14. _____   music + ian =   _____
15. _____   press + ure =   _____

Practice saying both the base words and the new words with the speaker on tape or with a partner. Check (√) the most difficult words and practice them with your class.

In this class you will be asked to monitor or to listen carefully to the following:

*1. **A classmate's pronunciation while she or he is speaking.** If you hear a pronunciation problem while monitoring a classmate, don't interrupt. Instead, make a note of the item that you think needs further practice and call it to the attention of your classmate after he or she has finished speaking. Give your classmates the opportunity to correct their own errors. Remember that pronunciation is a sensitive area for many learners of English!*

*2. **Your pronunciation while you are speaking.** If you hear a problem while you are speaking, correct it if the situation allows. If not, just note the problem and go on.*

*3. **Your pronunciation on audio- or videotape.** If you hear a problem on tape, stop the recorder. Rewind and listen again. Then try to correct the pronunciation yourself.*

When monitoring, focus on only one or two pronunciation points at a time. Listen for clear pronunciations, as well as unclear pronunciations.

Monitoring will be difficult at first but will become easier with practice. As your ability to monitor your classmates improves, your ability to self-monitor will get better also.

EXERCISE 3   With a partner, take turns reading the passage titled "American Government" in the section called *Listen*. Monitor your partner's pronunciation of the italicized letters.

Rule 3-5

Listen to the *qu* spelling pattern. Which sound(s) do you hear?

/k/ or /kw/?

qu- and -**qu**-

a **qu**alified applicant

a long e**qu**ation

outdated e**qu**ipment

in proper se**qu**ence

COMPLETE THE RULE: The -*qu*- and *qu*- spellings are pronounced like the **two** sounds /   /. (Pronunciation Hint: Round the lips for /w/ before you release the /k/ sound.)

Rule 3-6

Listen to the *x* and *cc* spelling patterns.   Do you hear one or two sounds? Circle the sound(s) you hear.

/s/ or /ks/?	*/s/ or /ks/?*
-x-	***-cc-*** *(before i and e)*
ex**cept** the teacher	ac**cept** the consequences
ex**cuse** me	suc**ceed** in business
a valuable ex**perience**	a serious ac**cident**
an ex**treme** position	ac**cess** to the informatiom

☑ COMPLETE THE RULE: The *-x-* and *-cc-* spellings are usually pronounced like the TWO sounds /   /.

> *Note:* The *-x-* in *exact, example, executive,* and *examine* is pronounced /gz/.

EXERCISE 4

Repeat the sentences below after your teacher or the speaker on tape or practice with a partner using the following procedure:

Example: Starter Phrase	*Completion Phrases*
That company *specializes* in	. . . office *furniture.*
	. . . *erosion* control.
	. . . *modular* homes.

• Student 2 closes the book.

• Student 1 gives Student 2 the starter phrase to memorize. Then Student 1 gives Student 2 the first completion phrase.

• Student 2 says the whole sentence: "That company specializes in office furniture."

• Student 1 gives Student 2 the next completion phrase.

• Student 2 says the same starter pattern with the next completion phrase: "That company specializes in erosion control." And so on . . .

Monitor your partner's pronunciation.

Starter Phrases	*Completion Phrases*
1. When is the next	quiz?
	quarterly report?
	qualifying exam?
	quality control meeting?
2. What is the situation with	the joint venture?
	our natural resources?
	the featured speaker?
	our future growth?
3. Those were excellent	decisions.
	revisions.
	audiovisuals.
	measurements.

(Switch Roles.)

4. When did we schedule	the graduation?
	the procedure?
	the in-service education?
	the graduate student meeting?
5. It'll require	efficiency.
	immediate action.
	special attention.*
	financial planning.

Rules and Practices 2: Final Consonant Sounds and Spellings

Final consonant sounds present special difficulty for many learners of English. Some students omit final consonants. They might say "bo- answer-" for "both answers." Other students confuse final voiceless and voiced consonants. They might say "Half a good day!" for "Have a good day!"

Final consonant sounds are either voiced—spoken with vocal cord vibration (/b/, /d/, /g/, /v/, /ð/, /z/, /ʒ/, /dʒ/, /m/, /n/, /ŋ/, /l/, /r/, /y/, /w/)—or voiceless—spoken without vocal cord vibration (/p/, /t/, /k/, /f/, /θ/, /s/, /ʃ/, /tʃ/, /h/). See Appendix B if you need a general review of voiced and voiceless consonants.

Sometimes spelling indicates whether a final consonant should be voiced or voiceless as in nee**d** and nea**t**; sometimes it does not, as in clo**se** /klo^{w}z / as a verb and clo**se** /klo^{w}s/ as an adjective. The following guidelines for final consonants will help make your speech clearer.

---

*When -**n**- precedes -**ti**- (atte**nti**on, preside**nti**al, crede**nti**als), the -**ti**- can be pronounced /ʃ/ as in **sh**oe or /tʃ/ as in **ch**oose.

Rule 3-7

Listen to the final voiceless and voiced consonants. See if you can detect the difference between them.

Voiceless	Voiced
safe	save
safe neighborhoods	save neighborhoods
white	wide
a white tie	a wide tie
price	prize
price increase	prize increase
lap	lab
lap computer	lab computer

What was the difference? In which column did the vowels sound longer?

✓ COMPLETE THE RULE: Vowels sound longer before final _____ _____ consonants.

Rule 3-8

The following word pairs are spelled the same but pronounced differently. What is the difference in pronunciation?

Noun or Adjective	Verb
use	use
close	close
excuse	excuse
abuse	abuse
diffuse	diffuse

In which column were the vowel sounds longer? In which column were the final consonants voiced?

✓ COMPLETE THE RULE: In the word pairs above, the final consonant is _____ in verbs and _____ in nouns/adjectives.

EXERCISE 5

Repeat the phrase pairs after the speaker on the tape or practice with your class. Listen carefully to your teacher. If your teacher says a phrase from the first column ("hou/s/e guests"), say the pair phrase from the second column ("hou/z/e guests"), and vice-versa.

Remember to l-e-n-g-t-h-e-n the vowels in the verb forms. Make an effort to blend the final consonant with the next word in each phrase.

Noun and Adjective Forms	*Verb Forms*
1. half_a cup_of coffee	have_a cup_of coffee
2. belief_in_yourself	believe_in_yourself
3. safe_money	save_money
4. advice_about_courses	advise_about_courses
5. relief_from_duties	relieve_from_duties
6. abuse_at_work	abuse_at_work
7. use_in_the kitchen	use_in_the kitchen
8. close_windows	close_windows
9. house_guests	house_guests
10. excuse_from_class	excuse_from class

EXERCISE 6

Listen carefully to your teacher or the speaker on the tape say each sentence twice. Did you hear the italicized word the first time (1) or the second time (2)? Circle 1 or 2.

Example:	1	②	That's a **wide** car.
1.	1	2	Have a **safe** trip.
2.	1	2	I **need** two pounds of fish.
3.	1	2	I can't **believe** it.
4.	1	2	Can you **prove** it?
5.	1	2	**Leave** the key at the desk.
6.	1	2	Your office is **close** to mine.
7.	1	2	Would you **close** the vent?
8.	1	2	Where's the first aid **kit**?
9.	1	2	**Excuse** me.
10.	1	2	I'll **have** a cup of coffee.

Check your answers with your teacher. With a partner, take turns saying the above sentences. Monitor your partner.

*H*ow do you address women in the United States?

Miss	=	/mɪs/, for unmarried women
Ms.	=	/mɪz/, for married or unmarried women
Missus (Mrs.)	=	/mɪsəz/, for married women

These titles are used before a woman's last or family name. Many women prefer the general title Ms. to Miss or Mrs. because Ms. can be used without regard to marital status. Ms. is also the correct title for a married woman who keeps her own name after marriage.

Listen to your teacher or the speaker on the tape say titles and names. Check *Married* if you hear Mrs., *Single* if you hear Miss, and *Don't know* if you hear Ms. Remember that Ms., with the final voiced /z/, will sound almost twice as long as Miss, with the final voiceless /s/.

	Married	Single	Don't know
Example			✔
1.			
2.			
3.			
4.			
5.			
6.			
7.			

Check your answers with your teacher.

EXERCISE 7   Read each situation silently and self-monitor your pronunciation of the italicized words. Then decide what you would say in each situation. Write your answers and share them with the class.

SITUATION A: You are working in a doctor's office. You have to call the ***next patient*** to go to ***examining*** room #1. The ***patient*** is a young female high school student. What will you say? ***Use*** an appropriate title and make up a name.

_____

_____

SITUATION B: You are a ticket agent for a major airline. You are assisting a family of two young children, a husband, and a wife who are flying to ***Portugal.*** You have checked the tickets and tagged the luggage for everyone in the family ***except*** for the woman. She is talking to her children and is not paying any ***attention*** to you. What will you say to her? ***Use*** a title and make up a name.

_____

_____

SITUATION C: Your company has just signed a contract to participate in a joint ***venture*** (a project involving two companies). The meeting has just ended. Everyone is walking around the room, shaking hands, ***congratulating*** each other, and talking about how optimistic they are about the project. You walk over to a woman whom you know from the other company. What will you say? ***Use*** a title and make up a name.

_____

_____

SITUATION D: You are a ***graduate*** student in ***architecture.**** Your faculty adviser is a woman with outstanding ***credentials*** (a Ph.D. from a top university in your field). You have an appointment with her. You arrive at her office on time. The door is open but she is working at her computer and doesn't know you are there. What will you say? ***Use*** a title and make up a name.

_____

_____

SITUATION E: Think of a time when you were in a ***situation*** in which you did not know how to address someone. Perhaps it was a person you didn't know. Share the ***situation*** with your teacher and classmates. Discuss possible ways to handle similar ***situations*** in the ***future.***

*The *ch* in these words sounds like /k/: architecture, chaos, chemical, chronic, cholera, stomachache, and chlorine.

Communicative Practice: Evacuate!

You are a member of a family living in a coastal area that is about to be struck by a hurricane. Your neighborhood must be evacuated to an elementary school that is farther inland. Families have just 15 minutes to get the things that they need from their homes. Each family includes a grandfather, a wife, a husband, a seven-year-old son, an eight-month-old daughter, and a pet cat.

Listed on page 39 are some things you might think about taking with you to the shelter. Rank the 10 things you would take in order of importance.

Step 1

Preview the pronunciation of the italicized sounds in these useful words and phrases:

We have to make a deci*si*on . . .

That's more essen*ti*al than . . .

We really nee*d* . . .

I don't think we'd u*s*e . . .

Preview the sound/spelling patterns in these words from the evacuation list: medica*ti*on, pre*ss*ure, finan*ci*al, televi*si*on, e*qu*ipment, e*x*tra, te*x*tbooks, and bo*x*.

Preview the final consonant sounds in these words from the evacuation list: ca*t*, foo*d*, fi*ve*, ai*d*, and ki*t*. Remember to make your vowels longer before final voiced consonants.

Step 2

Take five minutes and individually rank the 10 most important items in the order of their importance: 1 for most essential, 2 for second most essential, and so on.

Step 3

In the remaining 10 minutes, share your individual rankings in groups of four to five students. Try to reach agreement as a "family" about what to take. Report your top choices to the class.

Evacuation List*	Individual Ranking	Family Ranking
Ca*t*	_____	_____
Ca*t* foo*d*	_____	_____
Water dish for ca*t*	_____	_____
Grandfather's medica*ti*on for blood pre*ssu*re	_____	_____
E*x*tra change of clothes	_____	_____
Blankets	_____	_____
Portable televi*si*on	_____	_____
Baby foo*d*	_____	_____
Important finan*ci*al documents	_____	_____
Family photographs	_____	_____
Diapers	_____	_____
Outdoor cooking e*qu*ipment	_____	_____
Canned foo*d*	_____	_____
Games and books for recrea*ti*on	_____	_____
Cosmetics	_____	_____
Fi*v*e-gallon container of water	_____	_____
School te*x*tbooks	_____	_____
Soap and towels	_____	_____
Bo*x* of matches	_____	_____
First ai*d* ki*t*	_____	_____

*Adapted from Connie L. Shoemaker and F. Floyd Shoemaker, *Interactive Techniques for the ESL Classroom* (New York: Newbury House Publishers, 1991), pp. 128–129. Used with permission.

*U*nlearning old habits of speaking and learning new ones is difficult and sometimes tedious. These strategies will help make your out-of-class practice more effective:

1. Keep a list of difficult-to-pronounce words that you want to learn. Review them frequently.

2. Practice words in typical phrases and sentences you would say in real situations. Imagine you are an actor rehearsing before you go on stage.

3. Practice silently or in s-l-o-w m-o-t-i-o-n. Focus on the feel of the new sound.

4. Practice with your eyes closed. Focus on the sound of the new pattern.

5. Practice in front of a mirror. Imitate the facial positions and mouth movements of American English speakers. Clear English pronunciation requires active use of the mouth, lips, and jaw.

Oral Review: Sound and Spelling Patterns

Name _____

Record this review and submit the cassette to your teacher.

Oral paragraph reading is good preparation for the Test of Spoken English (TSE).

DIRECTIONS: You are a member of a nonprofit group that educates the public about the environment. A local radio station has donated broadcast time to your organization. You have been selected to tape the first announcement in a series of short public service broadcasts. Practice and then record the following:

Announcement:

"Good evening, everyone.

Earth Day 1990 called worldwide ***attention*** to the ***future*** of our environment. Many people ***believe*** that our planet faces serious threats and that we ***need*** to take immediate steps to ***save*** it. Here are some of the most serious environmental problems and some things ***individuals*** can do to make a difference.

Scientists are expressing concern about damage to the ozone layer caused by man-made gases escaping into the atmosphere. ***Erosion*** of the ozone layer has already resulted in increased rates of skin cancer from ***exposure*** to harmful rays of the sun. What can we do? Use air ***conditioners*** sparingly and avoid using plastic foam products like styrofoam cups.

Scientists are also ***expressing*** concern about the greenhouse effect, the ***gradual*** warming of the earth from the buildup of gases like carbon ***dioxide.*** The increase in ***temperatures*** would cause ***glaciers*** to melt and sea levels to rise. There would also be huge shifts in rainfall and ***agricultural*** patterns. What can we do? Buy energy ***efficient*** appliances and fuel ***efficient*** cars. Set thermostats in your homes to lower ***temperatures.***

The third problem is garbage overload and the ***contamination*** of groundwater. Many people are already addressing this ***issue*** by recycling newspapers, cans, glass, and plastic.

This was the first in our series of ***special*** announcements called "What on Earth Can We Do?" Help us with ***future*** broadcasts by telling us what **you** think the most pressing environmental ***issues*** are and what ordinary citizens like you are doing to ***assure*** environmental ***quality*** for the next ***generation.*** Call 222-2000 and leave a 90-second message on our 24-hour answering ***machine.***"

Listen to your tape before you submit it. Monitor your pronunciation of the italicized words. Make corrections at the end of the tape.

Syllables and Word Endings

Words in English have one or more syllables or beats. Listen to the words below. How many beats do you hear in each word?

1. act   active   actively   activity

2. vent   invent   invented   inventory

Now say the words with your teacher and tap the syllables or beats on your desk.

Learners of English sometimes add or omit syllables. Adding or omitting syllables can make words difficult to understand. In this chapter you will become more aware of the importance of syllables and word endings.

Listen!

LISTENING ACTIVITY 1

Listen to your teacher or the speaker on tape say one of the phrases from each pair. Mark the one that you hear.

1. ____ just find the answer   ____ justified the answer

2. ____ canned a salmon   ____ Canada salmon

3. ____ planned a garden   ____ planted a garden

4. ____ turned around   ____ turn it around

5. ____ considered answers   ____ considerate answers

6. ____ Miss Smith   ____ Mrs. Smith

7. ____ change the date   ____ change the data

8. ____ submit the report   ____ submitted the report

9. ____ drive the distance   ____ derive the distance

10. ____ gracious hosts   ____ gracious hostess

Check your answers with your teacher.

Listen again to your teacher or the speaker on tape say **both** phrases in each pair. See if you can identify the difference between the phrases in each set.

LISTENING ACTIVITY 2

Close your books and listen to your teacher or the speaker on tape present a short passage about color preference. The speaker will habitually omit an important feature of English grammar and pronunciation. Can you identify what is missing?*

How did this passage sound without -s endings? To an American English listener, omission of the final -s probably would **not** interfere with understanding, but it probably **would** interfere with the listener's ability to concentrate on what was being said.

Listen to the speaker read the passage correctly. Fill in the blanks below with the words that you hear. Notice how frequently -s endings occur in English.

Color Preference†

For many _____, _____ have been studying the _____ that influence human preference in _____.

Although the _____ are inconclusive, the _____ have been used to make _____ about _____ used in decorating and in the packaging of consumer _____.

One factor that _____ human preference in _____ is age. _____ are attracted to bright, warm _____, such as yellow and red. _____, on the other hand, prefer cool _____ like blue and green.

Economic _____ also influence color choice. For instance, in 1984, when the economy was in deep trouble, people preferred grey _____.

*Answer: Did you notice that all of the -s endings on nouns and verbs were missing?

†Information adapted from "The Blueing of America," *Time*, July 18, 1983, p. 62; Leslie Kane, "The Power of Color," *Health*, July 1982, p. 37; Birren Faber, *Selling Color to People* (New York: University Books, Inc., 1956).

In addition, where people live _____ color preference. Often a _____ home _____ a color break from the outside environment. The brown scenery in the southwest _____ little color, so _____ there have pink, orange, and other vibrant _____. In industrial _____ of the north, white _____ are preferred despite the industrial smoke and soot.

Finally, many _____ believe that personality _____ color choice. A person who _____ red is athletic and extroverted. Someone who _____ orange is friendly; a person who _____ pink is feminine and charming; a person who _____ blue may be intellectual and conservative; and a person who _____ purple is aristocratic and artistic.

Rules and Practices 1: Syllables and -*s* Endings

Rule 4-1

We pronounce -*s* endings on simple present tense verbs, plural nouns, and possessive nouns in three different ways.

Listen and write down what the -*s* ending sounds like in each group.

1. teach/teach**es**   office/offic**es**   George/George**'s**   =   ____

2. pay/pay**s**   read/read**s**   Laura/Laura**'s**   =   ____

3. fit/fit**s**   work/work**s**   Mark/Mark**'s**   =   ____

Compare your answers with the following rules.

☑ 1. In words that end in the hissing, sibilant sounds /s/, /z/, /ʃ/, /ʒ/, /tʃ/, and /dʒ/, like the words in group 1, the -*s* ending is spoken as an additional syllable /əz/ or /ɪz/.

☑ 2. In words ending in a voiced sound, like the words in group 2, the -*s* ending sounds like the voiced /z/ as in *zoo*.

☑ 3. In words ending in a voiceless sound, like the words in group 3, the -*s* ending sounds like the voiceless /s/ as in *so*.

EXERCISE 1

PART A: Say the word pairs below **with** your teacher or the speaker on tape. How many syllables are in each pair?

Final /əz/	*Final /z/*	*Final /s/*
fix/fixes	allow/allows	limit/limits
chance/chances	skill/skills	asset/assets
cause/causes	copy/copies	stock/stocks
_____	_____	_____
_____	_____	_____
_____	_____	_____

PART B: Add an -s ending to the following words and say them. Did you add the /z/, /s/, or the syllable /əz/? Write each word in the correct column above.

reference__, speech__, grade__, estimate__, intend__, erase__, plan__, laugh__,* result__

EXERCISE 2

PART A: Say the word pairs with the speaker on the tape or work with a partner as follows. If Student 1 says a word from column A, Student 2 says the pair word from Column B and vice-versa.

Example: If Student 1 says "chances,"
Student 2 says "chance."

A.	B.	A.	B.
chance	chances	count	county
page	pages	pick	picky
hosts	hostess	date	data
piece	pieces	quote	quota
match	matches	claps	collapse
notice	notices	prayed	parade
runway	runaway	state	estate

*The *gh* spelling at the end of words (laugh, enough, tough, cough) is usually pronounced as the voiceless /f/.

PART B: Say the statements and responses with the speakers on tape or practice with a partner as follows. Student 1 says one of the sentences in each pair. Student 2 gives the correct meaning/response. Students switch roles and repeat the exercise.

1. a. Our director had a big part.   (Yes. She was really involved.)

    b. Our director had a big party.   (Yes. She invited over 50 people.)

2. a. Did you forget to thank the
        hosts?   (No, I thanked them.)

    b. Did you forget to thank the
        hostess?   (No, I thanked her.)

3. a. Would you replace the fuse?   (I just put one in.)

    b. Would you replace the fuses?   (I just put some in.)

4. a. Do you have the date?   (It's on my calendar.)

    b. Do you have the data?   (It's being processed.)

5. a. He missed his chance to
        make up the test.   (And he had only one.)

    b. He missed his chances to
        make up the test.   (And he had three!)

6. a. The airline found your
        suitcase.   (Where was it?)

    b. The airline found your
        suitcases.   (Where were they?)

7. a. Her name is Miss Smith.   (Oh. Is she single?)

    b. Her name is Mrs. Smith.   (Oh. Is she married?)

EXERCISE 3   PART A: Circle the count nouns in the box below. Count nouns have singulars and plurals (key/keys, bus/buses). Noncount nouns have neither singular nor plural (homework, water). Note that some of the nouns, such as *time,* can be count or noncount depending on the context.

Check your answers with your teacher.

Practice the count nouns in both the singular and plural with the speaker on tape or with your teacher.

advantage	time	method	change
system	feedback	procedure	week
graph	possibility	input	approach
customer	consequence	case	increase
expense	experience	merchandise	invoice
branch	envelope	mail	homework
response	desk	conference	difference
luggage	assurance	reluctance	evidence

PART B: In this pair practice, Student 1 gives Student 2 the simple form of one of the words. Student 2 substitutes the word into one of the common phrases below, adding an *-s* ending when necessary.

Examples: Student 1 says "merchandise."

Student 2 says "a little merchandise."

Student 1 says "invoice."

Student 2 says "a few invoices."

Count Nouns	*Noncount Nouns*
not many _____	not much _____
a few _____	a little _____
a lot of _____	a lot of _____

Words with more than one final consonant sound, such as **test** and **direct,** are often difficult to pronounce. Adding a final -s increases the difficulty. Here are some pronunciation hints.

1. Many common words end in *-ct* (fact) and *-pt* (concept). When an *-s* is added, drop the *-t*: fac̸ts and concep̸ts.

Repeat these words and phrases. Make a smooth transition from the final *-s* to the next word in each phrase.

ct + s	*pt + s*
fact/fac̸ts	concept/concep̸ts
fac̸ts‿in the case	concep̸ts‿covered today
act/ac̸ts	adapt/adap̸ts
ac̸ts‿like he's mad	adap̸ts‿well
direct/direc̸ts	corrupt/corrup̸ts
direc̸ts‿traffic	corrup̸ts‿politicians
object/objec̸ts	attempt/attemp̸ts
objec̸ts‿strongly	attemp̸ts‿to save money

The *-ct+s* and *-pt+s* sequences can also occur across word boundaries.

Repeat these examples:

Voters will elec̸t city officials.

Deduc̸t seven dollars from the total.

They should accep̸t some of the blame.

2. When *-s* is added to words that end in *-st* (guest) and *-sk* (ask), the /t/ (gues̸ts) and /k/ (as̸ks) are often omitted in normal, rapid speech and the /s/ is lengthened.

Listen to the contrast between careful pronunciation and normal, rapid speech. The symbol (:) signals length.

a. Put the (desks/des:s) in the storage room.

b. I got the (lists/lis:s) of names.

c. She (asks/as:s) too many questions.

d. Have the (guests/gues:s) left?

e. I passed all of my (tests/tes:s) and quizzes.

Repeat each group of words below.

a. guess   guest   guest is   guests or gues:s

b. Tess   test   test is   tests or tes:s

c. chess   chest   chest is   chests or ches:s

The *st+s* sequences can also occur across word boundaries.

Repeat these examples.

Firefighting is the mos*t* stressful job I can think of.

She was the las*t* student to finish.

What's the bes*t* song on the tape?

Communicative Practice 1: Stockroom Inventory*

Practice plural nouns as you and your partner do a stockroom inventory. The *Stockroom Order Form* below has missing information. Your task is to complete the form and telephone the order to the stockroom manager.

Student 1 will work from Stock List A, and Student 2 will use Stock List B. Only part of the information you need is on each stock list, so you will need to share your data to complete the order form. Sit back to back; do not look at each other's stock lists.

Tape record your completed order to the stockroom manager. Listen to the tape and monitor your -*s* endings.

STOCKROOM ORDER FORM   DATE:_____

Items to be ordered: *Quantity:*

IBM computer monitors .... _____

IBM computer keyboards .... _____

Complete IBM computer sets... _____

Business software packages .... _____

TOEFL review books .... _____

Mechanical pencils .... _____

Art brushes .... _____

Spirit T-shirts .... _____

Texas Instruments scientific calculators .... _____

Pairs of sunglasses... _____

Pencil cases... _____

Calculus texts .... _____

Spirit watches .... _____

---

*Courtesy of David Miller, Instructor, Language Institute, Georgia Institute of Technology, Atlanta, Georgia

STOCK LIST A

Items to be ordered:	Currently In Stock	Target Inventory
IBM computer monitors......................	24	
IBM computer keyboards	41	43
Complete IBM computer sets..............		29
Business software packages..................		
TOEFL review books	36	
Mechanical pencils.............................		145
Art brushes...	74	
Spirit T-shirts.....................................		113
Scientific calculators...........................		
Pairs of sunglasses..............................	0	
Pencil cases	53	
Calculus texts......................................	281	500
Spirit watches.....................................		230

STOCK LIST B

Items to be ordered:	Currently In Stock	Target Inventory
IBM computer monitors		37
IBM computer keyboards		
Complete IBM computer sets	11	
Business software packages	19	19
TOEFL review books		60
Mechanical pencils	108	
Art brushes		70
Spirit T-shirts	113	
Scientific calculators	47	53
Pairs of sunglasses		250
Pencil cases		65
Calculus texts		
Spirit watches	193	

Rules and Practices 2: Syllables and *-ed* Endings

Rule 4-2

We pronounce the *-ed* ending on regular verbs in three different ways.

 Listen and write down what the *-ed* sounds like in the sentences below.

1. I project the profits.

   I project**ed** the profits.   = _____

2. The labs close at eight.

   The labs close**d** at eight.   = _____

3. They work at home.

   They work**ed** at home.   = _____

Compare your answers above with the following rules.

☑ 1. In verbs that end in /t/ or /d/, like projec**t**, the *-ed* is spoken as an extra syllable /əd/ or /ɪd/.

☑ 2. In verbs that end in voiced sounds, like clo**s**e as a verb, the *-ed* sounds like the voiced /d/ as in dime.

☑ 3. In verbs that end in voiceless sounds, like wor**k**, the *-ed* sounds like the voiceless /t/ as in time.

EXERCISE 4

PART A: Say the verb pairs below with your teacher or the speaker on tape. How many syllables are in each pair?

Final /əd/	*Final /d/*	*Final /t/*
construct/constructed	install/installed	talk/talked
decide/decided	save/saved	laugh/laughed
graduate/graduated	delay/delayed	process/processed
_____	_____	_____
_____	_____	_____
_____	_____	_____

PART B: Add an *-ed* to the following verbs and say them. Did you add the /d/, /t/, or the syllable /əd/? Write the words in the correct column above.

repeat____, crash____, turn____ on, provide____, plan____, produce____, analyze____, evaluate____, work____

Note: The *-ed* adjectives and the *-edly* adverbs add the syllable /əd/.

Examples: a wicked person   (wicked = 2 syllables)

           a naked baby   (naked = 2 syllables)

           supposedly accurate records   (supposedly = 4 syllables)

Your pronunciation of the past tense ending will sound more natural if you blend it or link it with the next word in the verb phrase. Even though you see white space between words on the page, do not separate the verb from the next word in the verb phrase.

Listen to these verb phrases and notice what happens when the word after the past tense ending begins with a vowel.

picked‿it up   (pick-ti-tup)

moved‿out   (move-dout)

fixed‿it   (fix-tit)

figured‿out   (figure-dout)

Listen to these verb phrases and notice what happens when the past tense ending is the same as or almost the same as the first sound in the next word.

planned‿to go   (sounds like *plan to go*)

narrowed‿down   (sounds like *narrow down*)

listened‿to   (sounds like *listen to*)

Listen to these verb phrases and notice what happens when the past tense ending resembles the sound that follows it.

changed‿the date   (sounds like *change the date*)

raised‿children   (sounds like *raise children*)

fixed‿the VCR   (sounds like *fix the VCR*)

EXERCISE 5

Practice past tense endings and link them with the next word in each verb phrase. After you say each sentence, listen to your teacher or the speaker on tape say the same sentence. Was yours correct?

1. He filled‿out the application.

2. The meeting's been called‿off.

3. I checked‿in this morning.

4. She's already checked‿out.

5. Have you narrowed‿down the possibilities?

6. The teacher has already handed‿our papers back.

7. He pointed‿out all of my mistakes.

8. That model will be gradually phased‿out.

9. I have already turned‿down three offers.

10. I've looked‿over your resume.

Which two past tense forms above were difficult to hear? Why?

Communicative Practice 2: Resume Worksheet

Practice past tense verb endings as you and your partner take turns collecting information for resumes.

Student 1 is a consultant who helps clients prepare resumes. The consultant's task is to obtain information about the client by asking questions and recording the information on the "Resume Work Sheet."

Student 2 is the client and should choose "Client Role A, B, C, or D" below and answer the consultant's questions as if in a real interview.

Preview the meanings and pronunciations of these key past tense verbs:

USEFUL PAST TENSE VERBS

started	coordinated	participated in
initiated	planned	owned
introduced	researched	volunteered
owned	analyzed	served
headed	evaluated	coached
managed	expanded	admitted
supervised	increased	attended
conducted	improved	graduated
administered	upgraded	obtained
organized	worked	

CLIENT ROLE A: You attended Ohio State University on a basketball scholarship and received a B.S. in sociology in 1974. Immediately thereafter, you enrolled in graduate school at the University of Maryland, where you received an M.B.A.

During graduate school you worked part-time at a flower concession and a laundromat. After graduate school, you served in the Peace Corps in Tanzania for five years. In late 1981, you were hired by an international consulting firm. During the early 1980s, you volunteered in an inner-city project tutoring African-American and Hispanic students in math and science.

You are now seeking work as a private consultant because you lost your job after a buyout of the international firm.

CLIENT ROLE B: You graduated from U.C.L.A. in 1978 with a B.S. in computer science and were recruited by a prestigious software firm where you worked 60–70 hours per week, developing software for hospitals and the health care system.

Three years later you had a child, at which time you started your own software development company and managed it from your home. You began the business as the sole employee, but within a year you added another full-time and two part-time employees. Now that your children are getting older, you have liquidated the business and are seeking another corporate position.

For the past year, you have served on the PTA (Parent Teacher Association) board at your child's school.

CLIENT ROLE C: You graduated from a Texas high school in 1982. Upon graduation, you enlisted in the army and served for two years. You then earned a degree in electronics from a two-year technical college.

You couldn't find work in electronics so you entered a training program for bank tellers with a local savings and loan. For the first year, you worked as a teller. The following year, you were promoted to head teller. The year after that, you moved to the credit department where you reviewed loan applications.

Last year, you were promoted to branch manager. Under your leadership, business at your branch has increased and you have expanded your work force from eight to ten employees.

There are rumors that the savings and loan parent company is experiencing serious financial difficulties so you are "playing it safe" and interviewing with other companies.

CLIENT ROLE D: Use your own career objective and educational and work history.

RESUME WORK SHEET

Name: _____

Address: _____

_____

Telephone Number: _____

Career Objective:_____

Education: (year graduated)   (degree)   (name of school)

  College   _____   _____   _____

               _____   _____   _____

  Technical Training

               _____   _____   _____

               _____   _____   _____

  High School (if no college)

               _____   _____   _____

Employment:

(years)   (position)   (duties and accomplishments)

_____   _____   _____

_____   _____   _____

_____   _____   _____

_____   _____   _____

Activities: (volunteer and civic involvements; outside interests; awards)

_____

_____

_____

_____

_____

_____

Note: The organization of a real resume will depend on the employment objective and experience of the individual.

Extend Your Skills . . . to Descriptions of Graphs

Explaining graphs is a useful academic and business skill. In this activity, you can practice using *-s* endings as you explain information presented in graph form.

Step 1

Preview the five parts of your explanation and practice useful phrases.

Part	*-s Forms in Useful Phrases*
a. Subject of the Graph	This graph show**s** . . . This graph illustrate**s** . . .
b. Components of the Graph	The *x* (horizontal) axis represent**s** . . . The *y* (vertical) axis indicate**s** . . .
c. Patterns	This graph demonstrate**s** . . . One of the trend**s** is . . . As ＿＿＿ increase**s**, . . . As ＿＿＿ decrease**s**, . . .
d. Example	For example, . . . For instance, . . .
e. Predictions or Implications	If this pattern (trend) continue**s** . . . If this trend hold**s** . . . One of the conclusion**s** is . . . One of the implication**s** is . . .

(When speaking of trends, increases, or decreases you may find terms like *slight(ly)*, *gradual(ly)*, *sharp(ly)*, *dramatic(ally)*, and *significant(ly)* useful.)

Step 2

Choose a graph from pages 60, 61, and 62 or find a simple one of interest in a magazine, textbook, or newspaper. Spend about five minutes outlining a short explanation of the graph. Present your explanation to the class or to a small group of five or six students. (Use notes or an outline, but do not read your explanation.) Be prepared to answer questions. Record your explanation on an audiocassette.

Step 3

After class, listen to your recording and evaluate your presentation on the *Explaining a Graph Self-Evaluation Form*. Submit your evaluation to your instructor.

Figure 4-1

Life expectancy at birth,
by race and sex: 1900–1986*

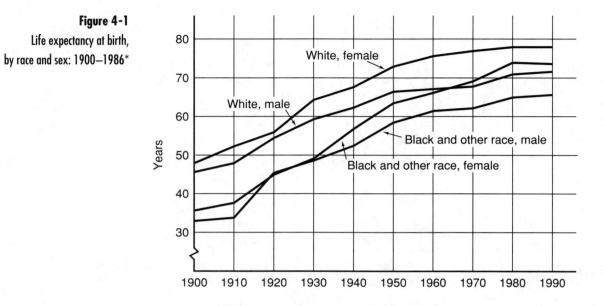

*Sources: U.S. Department of Health, Education, and Welfare, Public Health Service, National Center for Health Statistics, *Vital Statistics of the United States 1973*, Vol. 2, part A, section 5, and data in preparation; *Statistical Abstract of the United States: 1990*, U.S. Department of the Census, Bureau of the Census, p. 74.

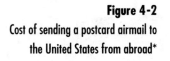

Figure 4-2

Cost of sending a postcard airmail to
the United States from abroad*

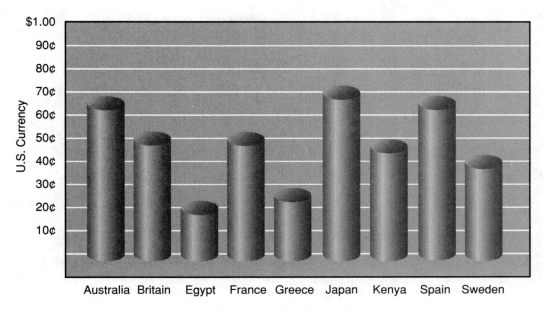

*Source of data: *New York Times,* Sunday, August 4, 1991, p. 3.

Figure 4-3

Average hours per week the American eighth grader spends on various activities*

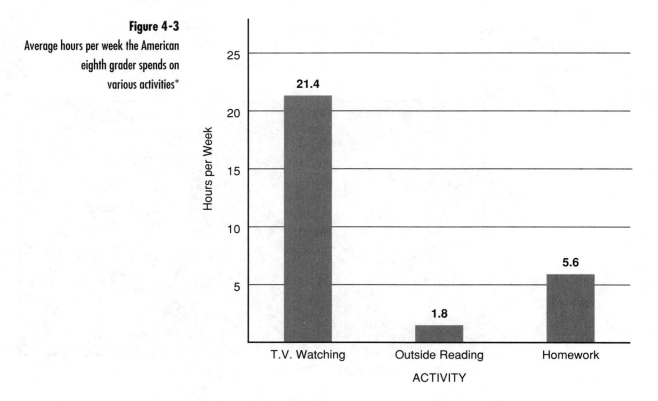

*Source: U.S. Department of Education, National Center for Education Statistics, *Profile of the American Eighth Grader: NELS: 88 Student Descriptive Summary.* June 1990, p. 48.

EXPLAINING A GRAPH/SELF-EVALUATION FORM

Name_____

PART I. Listen to your your tape. Write down every noun and verb with an *-s* ending.

PART II. Assign one point for each component below. You might need to listen to your tape several times.

A. Clarity of Organization	1 point each	
1. Subject clearly stated	_____	
2. Components identified	_____	
3. Patterns identified	_____	
4. One example given	_____	
5. End clearly indicated	_____	
Total (Part A)	_____ × 10 =	
_____		
B. Clarity of Speech	1 point each	
1. Adequate volume	_____	
2. Good speed	_____	
3. Clear pronunciation of key words	_____	
4. Final *-s* about 75% correct	_____	
5. Good overall clarity	_____	
Total (Part B)	_____ × 10 =	
_____		

Total (Part A + B)
_____%

Comments:

Oral Review: Syllables and Word Endings

Schedule an individual consultation with your instructor, complete the review as a group project, or submit the review on tape.

Complete each statement orally. Do not write and then read your sentence completions.

Sentence completion practice is good preparation for the Test of Spoken English (TSE).

1. AIDS was discovered in the early 1980s. Since then, . . .

2. My adviser never arranges meetings between 9:00 A.M. and 5:00 P.M.; he usually . . .

3. After he exercises, he always takes a shower and . . .

4. I have already picked up John at the airport three times this month. The next time he . . .

5. While the offices are being painted, everyone . . .

6. In a recent survey, parents predicted yearly costs at a four-year public college to be about $7,000. Actual costs averaged about $2,000 a year. The costs were about $5,000 lower than . . .

7. A typical professor in a university in the United States expects students to ask questions and participate in discussions. A professor in my country . . .

8. When the Berlin Wall was demolished, people of all ages . . .

9. I was wrong. I didn't think the rent included any utilities, but it . . .

10. I have been confused many times in the United States, but I was most confused the time that . . .

Rewind your tape. Monitor your word endings. Make corrections at the end of your tape.

Stress in Words (Part 1)

In every word of two or more syllables, one of the syllables is stronger than the others. Notice the strongest or STRESSED syllable in each of the following words:

FI nal   pro FES sor   dem o CRAT ic   vo CAB u lar y

What makes a syllable sound stressed or emphasized in American English? A combination of these three features creates syllable stress.

- **Length:** The vowel in the stressed syllable is longer. Which vowel sound is the longest in *meth od*?

- **Pitch:** The stressed syllable has a higher pitch. Which syllable has the higher pitch in *ap peal*?

- **Clear Vowel:** The stressed syllable has a full, clear vowel. Which syllable has the full, clear vowel in *ca pa ble*?

Vowels in unstressed syllables are weak or reduced. They often sound like the neutral vowel sound /ə/ as in *a*bout.

    Why is syllable stress important? Speakers of English rely on patterns of stress to help them identify the words they hear. The more frequently you misuse stress, the more effort listeners have to make to understand what you are saying.
    The next two chapters will help you improve your ability to predict and use stress patterns in words.

Listen!

LISTENING ACTIVITY 1

Listen to the speaker on tape or your teacher say one of the words from each pair. Put a check next to the word that you hear.

1. ____ greenhouse   ____ green house

2. ____ breakfast   ____ break fast

3. ____ differentiated   ____ different shaded

4. ____ decade   ____ decayed

5. ____ pronouns   ____ pronounce

6. ____ orders   ____ hors d'oeuvres

7. ____ often   ____ offend

8. ____ offer   ____ a fur

9. ____ one person   ____ one percent

10. ____ lookout   ____ Look out!

Check your answers with your teacher.

Now listen to **both** items in each pair. Can you hear the difference between them?

Drawing by Randy Wicks, © *The Newhall Signal*, 1990. Reprinted by permission of Rothco Cartoons.

LISTENING ACTIVITY 2

Ask an American English speaker to say the words below (or listen carefully to the speaker on the tape). Underline the syllable (or the vowel) that is longer, clearer, and higher in pitch. Check your answers with your teacher.

Suggestion: If you ask a native speaker to say the words in sentences, the pronunciation will probably sound more natural.

Example: pessi<u>mi</u>stic

1. volunteer
2. himself
3. survey (noun)
4. increase (noun)
5. recall (verb)
6. software
7. air conditioner

8. economy
9. economical
10. electricity
11. electrical
12. estimate
13. estimating
14. estimated

Note: Some words with more than one syllable have more than one stress. In the word *university,* the third ("ver") syllable has the strongest or the primary stress. The first ("u") syllable has a weaker or a secondary stress. In clear speaking, the primary stress in each word is the most important.

LISTENING ACTIVITY 3

Listen to your teacher or the speaker on tape say the following words. Focus your attention on the *un*stressed syllables which are **not** capitalized. The unstressed syllables are shorter, softer, lower in pitch, and often said with the schwa vowel sound /ə/ as in *a*bout.

Each time you hear the neutral /ə/ sound, put a line through the vowel.

Examples: METH ~~o~~d

com PUTE

bi ~~o~~ LOG i c~~a~~l

1. con SULT ant
2. IN dus try
3. pro FES sion al
4. com MU ni ty
5. col LECT ed

6. CON fi denc es
7. po LIT i cal
8. de LI cious
9. DEM on strate
10. a POL o gize

Check your answers in your dictionary. Notice that not all unstressed vowels sound like schwa /ə/, but many do.

Note: Some English speakers use /ə/ and others use /ɪ/ in unstressed syllables. In the fourth syllable of the word biological, the -i- can be /ə/ or /ɪ/. Similarly, the *-ed* syllable in the word collected can be /əd/ or /ɪd/.

Rules and Practices: Using Parts of Speech to Predict Stress

Many words in English have no systematic rules for stressed and unstressed syllables. Others have rules that are too complicated to be useful.

However, you **can** sometimes determine where stress falls in a word based on its part of speech. In other words, recognizing that a word is a noun, verb, adverb, or pronoun can sometimes help you know which syllable to stress.

The following guidelines will help you predict stress in words. Remember these are guidelines and no rule is infallible!

Rule 5-1

Listen to the stress in compound nouns. Can you identify a pattern?

deadline	establish a deadline
classroom	a noisy classroom
software	software packages
steakhouse	a Japanese steakhouse

☑ Stress the first part of the compound.

Example: AIRport

Note: Two-syllable nouns with a prefix are much like compound nouns. Stress the prefix.

Examples: INcome, BYlaws

Rule 5-2

Listen to these noun + noun combinations. Where is the stress?

air conditioner   repair the air conditioner

shoe polish   some brown shoe polish

convention center   the downtown convention center

✓ The stress often falls on the first noun or the stressed syllable of the first noun.

Examples: TOOTH decay, VAcuum cleaner, comPUter center

Rule 5-3

Listen to these reflexive pronouns. Where is the stress?

myself   went by myself

themselves   finished it themselves

✓ Stress the *-self* or *-selves* syllable.

Example: herSELF

Rule 5-4

Listen to the numbers like *fourteen* and *forty*. Do you hear a regular pattern of stress?

thirteen years old / thirty years old

sixteen dollars / sixty dollars

✓ Stress the *-teen* syllable.

Example: eighTEEN vs. EIGHty

EXERCISE 1

Say the following compound nouns and noun + noun combinations with the speaker on tape or take turns saying them with a partner.

Remember to s-t-r-e-t-c-h or prolong your stressed syllables. Length is the **most** important feature of stress.

Examples: C-O-C-Kpit

R-E-S-Troom

W-O-R-D processor

businessman	earthquake	teenager
greenhouse	airmail	classroom
workbook	headache	roommate
outline		

seat belt	television station	fire extinguisher
stock market	bank account	credit card
sports car	air bag	

Choose three compound nouns or noun + noun combinations that you use frequently and write typical sentences you might say with them. Dictate your sentences to your partner.

1._____

2._____

3._____

Rule 5-5

Listen to the verbs consisting of a prefix and a one-syllable base. Can you identify the stress pattern?

outrun	outrun his teammate
overlook	overlook the error
withdraw	withdrew fifty dollars
overhear	overheard the argument

✓ Stress the base of these verbs.

Example: underSTAND

Rule 5-6

Listen to the stress patterns in two-word verbs. Where is the stress?

print out	print out the document
shut down	shut down the factory
put off	put off the meeting

 Stress the last or prepositional component.

Example: give UP

Practice these two-word verbs. Remember to use correct past tense *-ed* endings and linking.

passed out	narrowed down
pointed out	figured out
dropped off	

> *Note:* Sometimes two-word verbs have noun equivalents. In the noun forms, the stress falls on the first part of the two-word verb.

Noun: Here's the *PRINTout.*   Verb: I *printed* it *OUT.*

Noun: She's a *DROPout.*   Verb: She *dropped OUT.*

Rule 5-7

Listen to these compound adverbs indicating location or direction. Where is the stress?

overseas	go overseas
downtown	drove downtown
northeast	in the northeast

 Stress the second part of the compound in adverbs.

Example: outSIDE

Rule 5-8

Listen to these two-syllable words used as both nouns and verbs. Can you hear a pattern in the placement of stress?

Noun	Verb
conduct	conduct
present	present
project	project
rebel	rebel

✓ Stress the first syllable in nouns (INsult) and the second syllable in verbs (inSULT).

Listen to the noun-verb pairs once more. What happened to the vowel sound in the first syllable of each verb?

THINK ABOUT WHAT YOU HAVE LEARNED

Can you create a general rule for stress in nouns?

Can you create a general rule for stress in verbs?

EXERCISE 2

Say the following noun-verb pairs with the speaker on tape or work with a partner as follows. Student 1 says one of the words from each of the noun-verb pairs. If Student 1 uses a noun stress pattern, Student 2 should say the same word with the verb stress pattern and vice-versa.

Noun	Verb
convert	convert
conduct	conduct
insult	insult
progress	progress
object	object
project	project
survey	survey
suspect	suspect

Noun	Verb
upset	upset
recall	recall
checkout	check out
turnover	turn over
handout	hand out
follow-up	follow up
takeover	take over
makeup	make up

Note: Sometimes the meanings of the noun-verb pairs are unrelated as in *OBject-obJECT* and *DEsert-deSERT*. Look up any words you are unsure of in your dictionary.

EXERCISE 3

Say the words and sentences below. After you say each sentence, listen to your teacher or the speaker on the tape say the same sentence. Were your stress patterns correct?

1. (pay back)   I'll pay you back after my next paycheck.

2. (paycheck)   I'll pay you back after my next paycheck.

3. (newspaper)   Recycling newspaper is a good idea.

4. (checkbook)   My checkbook is missing.

5. (dropout)   He's a college dropout.

6. (overthrow)   The military tried to overthrow the government.

7. (upside-down)   The car turned upside-down.

8. (give up)   Don't give up before you try.

9. (present)   She's going to present the speaker.

10. (permit)   You'll need a permit to do the construction.

11. (suspect)   The police arrested the suspect.

12. (girlfriend/fourteen)   John's girlfriend just turned fourteen.

13. (pick up/fifty)   Pick me up at 7:50.

14. (project)   Can you project our profits for the next quarter?

15. (hand in/homework)   Hand in your homework at the end of class.

*W*hen *we say abbreviations and symbols for elements and compounds, all letters and numbers have full stresses. The pitch glides down on the final letter or number.*

Example: M A ↘ (Master of Arts)

F B I ↘ (Federal Bureau of Investigation)

If a speaker says three or more stressed syllables in sequence, the rate of speech slows significantly.

Examples: M B A   P O W   L P N

EXERCISE 4   Write the abbreviations and symbols for the following places, organizations, elements, and compounds.

Say each abbreviation and then listen to the speaker on the tape say it. Or take turns saying the abbreviations with a partner. Monitor your partner.

1. _____ Trans World Airlines

2. _____ World Health Organization

3. _____ water

4. _____ sodium

5. _____ carbon dioxide

6. _____ International Business Machines

7. _____ Certified Public Accountant

8. _____ Environmental Protection Agency

9. _____ Very Important Person

10. _____ Chief Executive Officer

11. _____ Grade Point Average

12. _____ United Arab Emirates

13. _____ Music Television Video

14. _____ Automatic Teller Machine

15. _____ Cardiopulmonary Resuscitation

Add some of your own.

16. _____ _____

17. _____ _____

18. _____ _____

Communicative Practice: Giving an Explanation

Choose one of the following topics. Spend approximately two minutes creating and rehearsing a two- to three-minute explanation. Pay particular attention to the stress patterns in nouns and verbs. Present your explanation to a small group. Transition words like *first, second, next, after that,* and *finally* will help make your explanation clearer.

SUGGESTION: If you record your explanation, you can judge the accuracy of stress patterns on the tape.

TOPIC A. Explain to someone who usually uses a typewriter how to write a letter on a word processor.

Preview key vocabulary that is likely to occur in your explanation: turn on, turn off, type in, pick out, get through, print out, printout, insert, put in, word processor, and software. Note that *print out* as a verb and *printout* as a noun will have different stress patterns.

TOPIC B. Explain the procedure for checking out books from a particular library.

Preview key vocabulary that is likely to appear in your explanation: go in, pick out, take (the books) over, go over (to the desk), check out, take out, go out, permit, library card, and identification card.

TOPIC C. Discuss the household chores and errands you have to do this weekend.

Preview key vocabulary: housework, weekend, clean up, put away, hang up, drop off, call up, throw away, take out, and pick up.

Extend Your Skills . . . to Problem Solving

You have just received a notice from your bank, National Bank of Illinois (NBI), stating that there are insufficient funds in your account to cover the most recent check received. Your records, which are somewhat incomplete, indicate that you had enough money in your account. Call the bank and determine where the error lies.

You, the customer, have your checkbook. Your partner, the bank officer, has the printout of your canceled checks on the following page. Compare your records item by item and fill in any missing information. Remember this is a phone conversation and you cannot see each other's records.

Preview stress patterns in key terms. Lengthen the stressed syllables:

AT&T	drugstore	traffic court	sixty
NBI	MasterCard	money order	fifteen
	haircut	pet store	thirteen
	bookstore	dog food	thirty
	payment	service charge	forty
	textbooks	check number	
		account number	

Name:
Account Number 113-980-614-3

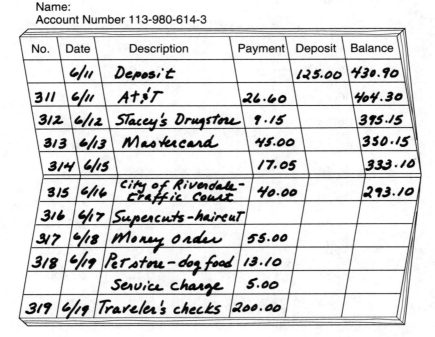

No.	Date	Description	Payment	Deposit	Balance
	6/11	Deposit		125.00	430.90
311	6/11	At$T	26.60		404.30
312	6/12	Stacey's Drugstore	9.15		395.15
313	6/13	Mastercard	45.00		350.15
314	6/15		17.05		333.10
315	6/16	City of Rivendale - traffic Court	40.00		293.10
316	6/17	Supercuts - haircut			
317	6/18	Money Order	55.00		
318	6/19	Pet store - dog food	13.10		
		Service charge	5.00		
319	6/19	Traveler's checks	200.00		

National Bank of Illinois (NBI)

2000 Riverside Parkway

Riverdale

****

Name_____

Account Number 113 980 614 3

                    - CHECKS POSTED -

DATE	CHECK NUMBER	AMOUNT	BALANCE
06-11	Deposit	125.00	430.90
06-15	311	26.60	404.30
06-16	312	9.15	395.15
06-17	313	45.00	350.15
06-19	314*	17.05	333.10
06-20	315	40.00	293.10
06-21	316	8.00	285.10
06-22	317	55.00	230.10
06-23	318	30.10	200.00
06-23	Service Chg.	5.00	195.00
06-23	319	200.00	– 5.00

– –

*Check number 314 was written to Cambridge Bookstore for textbooks,
according to the canceled check.

(The oral review for stress in words appears at the end of Chapter 6.)

Stress in Words (Part 2)

In Chapter 5 you used parts of speech to predict stress in words. Another way to predict stress is to use suffixes or word endings. Many common suffixes like *-ity, -ic,* and *-ogy,* when added to the ends of words, create predictable patterns of word stress.

Listen to your teacher say the sets of words below. Can you hear a regular pattern of stress in each set?

1. facility   credibility   minority   objectivity

2. athletic   traumatic   historic   atomic

3. guarantee   referee   absentee   trainee

In this chapter you will learn some general guidelines for suffixes and word stress. These guidelines will help you pronounce new words accurately. The guidelines are especially useful for pronouncing long academic, scientific, and technical terms that come from Latin and Greek.

Listen!

LISTENING ACTIVITY 1

Listen to your teacher or the speaker on the tape read the passage two times. The first time, close your book and listen for meaning. The second time, write the missing words in the spaces below.

The Challenger Disaster: Assessing the Implications*

When the space shuttle Challenger exploded in the blue Florida sky last week, killing all seven crew members, it underscored not only the _____ of human life but the _____ of human _____. Thus, as the nation paid tribute to the Challenger astronauts, and as _____ of the National _____ and Space _____ (NASA) pursued their _____ into the cause of the disaster, policymakers back in Washington were moving toward a careful reassessment of the nation's near total dependence on the shuttle for access to space.

Obviously, the most urgent _____ is to find out what happened; until NASA _____ know that, they have no way of knowing how long the rest of the shuttle fleet will be grounded, nor can they say how long it will take and how much it will cost to fix the problem.

As *Science* went to press, agency _____ were still refusing to _____ as to the cause of the _____. However, on Saturday, 1 February, at a meeting with members and staffers of the _____ space committees at NASA headquarters in Washington, acting _____ William Graham showed previously unreleased photographs that revealed an abnormal white spot of light—Graham declined to call it a flame—appearing on the right-hand solid rocket booster about 10 seconds before the _____ and about one-third of the way from the bottom of the booster. The light continued to spread along the right side until the instant of _____, at which point the liquid hydrogen and liquid oxygen fuel stored in the external tank exploded and consumed both Challenger and its crew.

Check your answers with your teacher.

*From M. Mitchell Waldrop, "The Challenger Disaster: Assessing the Implications," *Science* 231, February 14, 1986, pp. 661–663. Copyright 1986 by the AAAS. Reprinted by permission.

Rules and Practices: Using Suffixes to Predict Stress

Rule 6-1

The stress pattern for all the suffixes below is the same. Listen to the words or say the words along with your teacher or the speaker on the tape. See if you can identify the pattern.

-ic	*-ical*	*-ity*
scientific	economical	publicity
electronic	technological	fatality
chaotic	neurological	humanity
-ify	*-ogy*	*-ion*
solidify	anthropology	distribution
personify	psychology	manipulation
humidify	microbiology	expression
-scopy	*-meter*	*-graphy*
microscopy	kilometer	photography
telescopy	parameter	pornography
fluoroscopy	tachometer	biography

✓ Stress the syllable **before** each of the suffixes above.

Examples: optiMIStic, eligiBILity, psyCHOLogy

Rule 6-2

Listen to the words with suffixes like *-ee, -eer, -ese, -esce, -esque,* and *-ette.* What is the stress pattern?

volunteer	a volunteer effort
referee	referee the game
diskette	high-density diskette
Japanese	Japanese students

✓ Stress the syllable **with** each of the suffixes above.

Examples: engiNEER, bruNETTE

EXERCISE 1   Create new parts of speech with the following words by adding one or more of the suffixes *-ee, -ese, -ic, -ical, -ify, -ity, -ion,* and *-ogy*. Underline the syllable (or simply the vowel) with the primary stress in each word.

Compare your answers with those of your partner. Take turns saying the original words and the new words. Monitor your partner.

	Noun	*Verb*	*Adjective*
Examples: p<u>e</u>riod	perio<u>di</u>city		peri<u>o</u>dic
e<u>co</u>nomy	e<u>co</u>nomy/ eco<u>no</u>mics	e<u>co</u>nomize	eco<u>no</u>mic/ eco<u>no</u>mical
1. electric			
2. alcohol			
3. person			
4. major			
5. method			
6. photograph			
7. Japan			
8. absent			
9. philosophy			
10. mechanism			

Rule 6-3

Approximately 1,000 English verbs end in *-ate*. These verbs are used frequently in scientific, academic, and business settings and they have predictable stress patterns.

Listen to your teacher or the speaker on tape say these verbs. Can you identify a pattern?

exaggerate	associate	procrastinate
integrate	duplicate	accumulate

☑ Many learners of American English stress the *-ate* syllable. However, the third syllable from the end should be stressed (EStimate), even if an *-ed* (EStimated) or an *-ing* (EStimating) is added. The only time the stress shifts to another syllable is if *-ion* is added (estiMAtion). With practice this pattern will become natural.

Repeat these examples:

EStimate	EStimated	EStimating	EStimator	(estiMAtion)
indicate	indicated	indicating	indicator	(indication)
coordinate	coordinated	coordinating	coordinator	(coordination)

EXERCISE 2

Fill in the following word grid.

Practice saying the words. Check your pronunciation with the speaker on tape or have your partner monitor you. Remember to l-e-n-g-t-h-e-n the stressed syllables.

Verb	*Add* -ed	*Add* -ing	*Noun or Adj.*	*Add* -ion
Examples: rotate	rotated	rotating	————	rotation
associate	associated	associating	associate	association
1. demonstrate				
2. graduate				
3. differentiate				
4. alternate				
5. separate				

Sometimes -ate words are adjectives, nouns, and adverbs, as well as verbs.

Example of an adjective: That's an **accurate** *description.*

Example of a noun: She's a **graduate** *of M.I.T.*

Example of an adverb: Send the order **immediately.**

In adjectives, noun, and adverb forms, the stress pattern is the same, but the **-ate** *syllable sounds like the word* **it.**

NOUN
Here is a DUplicate of the letter.
        *(-ate = **it**)*

VERB
I need to DUplicate the letter.
        *(-ate = **ate**)*

NOUN
He's going to give us an EStimate.
                *(-ate = **it**)*

VERB
He's going to EStimate the cost.
        *(-ate = **ate**)*

EXERCISE 3   With a partner, apply what you know about stress patterns and say the words below. Then take turns using the words to create meaningful sentences. Monitor your partner for stress and for *-s* and *-ed* word endings.

Example: concept / illustrate / handout

        The concept is illustrated in your handout.

  1. what / equation / demonstrate

  2. how / Japanese / American / management style / different

  3. classmates / graduate / June fifteenth

  4. after / graduate / continue / education / graduate student

  5. atomic / power / result / years / technological / research

  6. majority / Democratic / delegate / vote / Jimmy Carter

  7. name / associate professor / economics

  8. Challenger / explosion / underscore / vulnerability / technology

  9. official / refuse / speculate / cause / disaster

 10. airplane / miss / runway

Communicative Practice 1: Reading an Announcement

In this pair practice, use what you know about stress and sound/spelling patterns to pronounce long, difficult words you might be seeing for the first time.

Imagine that you are talking to a colleague (your partner) on the telephone. Use the following announcement to give your partner specific information about a conference. Your partner should write down the information as you give it and indicate to you with "uh-huh" or "okay" when he or she is ready for the next piece of information. Sit back to back so you will have to communicate by speaking only.

When you have finished, your partner can compare his or her notes with the announcement.

Converting a written schedule into a spoken message is good preparation for the Test of Spoken English (TSE).

BIOMEDICAL TECHNOLOGY RESEARCH CENTER
Fourth Annual Convocation
Wednesday, April 16

3:30   Keynote Address
        "Preparing Your Research for Patentability"

        Seed Grant Investigators' Reports
        1. "The Cone Electrode and Potential Prosthetic Applications"
        2. "How to Regulate Neuromodulators"
        3. "Corneal Biomechanics"

5:30   Reception   Ballroom

Communicative Practice 2: Library Orientation

In this library orientation activity, one partner has the key (below) to the location of various areas of the library on the three floors. The other partner has a map of the library (on the next page) with only a letter designating each area.

First, ask your partner to look at the list of areas under the map and to tell you the eight to ten areas of greatest interest. Circle your partner's areas of interest on your key to location.

Then give the location of each area of interest by floor and letter to your partner. Your partner should write each area of interest in the appropriate blank on the map.

KEY TO LOCATION

First Floor	*Second Floor*	*Third Floor*
A. Circulation	F. CDs/Cassettes	L. Education
B. Periodicals/ Foreign Newspapers	G. Photography	M. Anthropology
C. Restrooms	H. Handicrafts	N. Political Science
D. Fire Exit	I. Psychology	O. Cookbooks
E. Catalog/ Terminals	J. Biography	P. Mathematics
	K. Biological Sciences	Q. Engineering

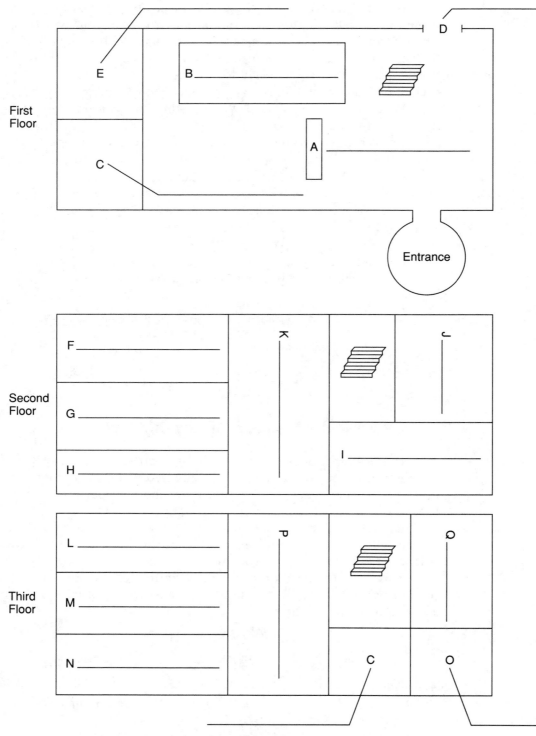

First
Floor

E

B _____

D

A _____

C _____

Entrance

Second
Floor

F _____

G _____

H _____

K

J

I _____

Third
Floor

L _____

M _____

N _____

P

Q

C

O

Choose eight to ten areas of greatest interest:
Restrooms   Fire Exit   Circulation (check out)
Catalogs/Terminals Foreign Newspapers/Periodicals
Education   Engineering   Anthropology   Mathematics
Photography   CDs and Cassettes   Biography
Psychology   Cookbooks   Handicrafts
Political Science   Biological Sciences

Extend Your Skills . . . to Small Group Discussions

DISCUSSION: You are a member of the International Olympic Committee. It is your job to select a suitable city for the next Summer Olympics.

Arrange yourselves in groups of four or five. Each person in your group should select his or her favorite city in the world to be the choice for hosting the next Olympics. Write your choice and the choices of the other group members in the chart on the next page.

As you work through the categories on the chart, evaluate the city of your choice on a scale of 1–5: 5–excellent; 4–good; 3–average; 2–fair; 1–poor. Discuss and defend your ratings as you work through the categories. Add up total points (maximum score is 50) and try to reach consensus on the best candidate.

Preview the stress patterns in key terms: Remember that your stressed syllables need l-e-n-g-t-h.

airport	night clubs	accessibility	accommodations
airlines	table tennis	quality	transportation
baseball	water polo	stability	
basketball	taxicab	security	
volleyball	street crime	humidity	
freeways		hospitality	
subways			
forecast			
weightlifting			

5 = excellent   4 = good   3 = average   2 = fair   1 = poor

Categories and Comments	Your City	(name of city) 1	(name of city) 2	(name of city) 3	(name of city) 4
Accessibility—Airport/airlines:					
Accommodations—Number/quality of hotel rooms:					
Transportation—Freeways/subways/taxicabs:					
Entertainment—Restaurants/night clubs:					
Sports Facilities—For swimming, track, baseball, basketball, volleyball, table tennis, water polo, field hockey, sailing, weightlifting, etc.:					
Languages—Number spoken:					
Political Stability of Country:					
Security—Street crime/police force:					
Weather—July forecast/humidity:					
Other—Corporate support/hospitality/medical facilities/other unique aspects of the city:					
TOTAL SCORES					

Adapted from chart by staff accompanying "Grading the Competition: Atlanta," *Atlanta Journal and Constitution,* July 15, 1990, p. A–1.   Reprinted with permission from the *Atlanta Journal* and the *Atlanta Constitution.*

Summarize your group's bid on the following "Outline for Bid." Select a spokesperson to present the bid to the class in two minutes or less.

As you present the strengths, introduce each new category with transition words and phrases, such as *one positive point, next,* and *in addition.* See the outline form for a complete list of useful transitions.

Be sure to provide specific examples to make your bid interesting. For example, if your city received a rating of **excellent** in languages spoken, mention the languages spoken in that city.

In your summary, you might indicate that you have fully considered your choice by mentioning one weak area. However, finish your summary with another mention of the one or two greatest strengths. Your listeners are likely to remember what they hear last. The class can select the most convincing presentation.

OUTLINE FOR BID

Useful Phrases

We'd like to nominate . . . Our candidate for . . .	Top candidate: Points: 1. _____ _____
First . . . One positive point . . . Next . . . In addition . . . Another positive point . . . The greatest strength . . . Finally . . .	Strengths: 1. 2. 3. 4. 5.
In summary . . . In conclusion . . . In closing . . .	Summary: 1. One weakness: 2. Two greatest strengths:

Oral Review: Stress in Words

Name _____

Schedule an individual consultation with your instructor, complete the review as a group project, or submit the review on tape.

Part A

Say the sentences. Pay attention to the stress patterns in the underlined words.

1. He has a high <u>metabolic</u> rate.

2. You'll get a <u>certificate</u> when you complete the course.

3. That's the <u>suspect</u>.

4. He's <u>suspected</u> of forgery.

5. We plan to <u>present</u> an award to her.

6. I can't <u>figure</u> it <u>out</u> by <u>myself</u>.

7. You're not <u>permitted</u> to park here without a <u>permit</u>.

8. We expect an <u>increase</u> in salary.

9. John is one of the new <u>corporate</u> officers.

10. He's working on a <u>degree</u> in <u>pharmacology</u>.

Part B

Record yourself reading the "Challenger Disaster" passage in *Listening Activity 1* at the beginning of the chapter.

Rewind your tape and listen to it. Monitor your stress patterns. Were your stressed syllables longer than your unstressed syllables? Make corrections at the end of your tape.

Mid-Course Self-Evaluation

Part A:

Circle the Answers   (1 = not at all . . . 5 = very much).

1. My general awareness of English speech patterns has improved.   1   2   3   4   5

2. I have a better idea of why I am sometimes not understood.   1   2   3   4   5

3. I am beginning to hear problems in my own speech.   1   2   3   4   5

4. My speech is beginning to improve.   1   2   3   4   5

5. I want to improve my intelligibility.   1   2   3   4   5

6. I have worked hard to improve my intelligibility.   1   2   3   4   5

Part B:

Answer the questions.

1. In what ways has my speech improved?

2. What are the three main areas in which I would like my speech to improve before the end of the course?

    a.

    b.

    c.

3. What will I have to do to achieve these changes in my speech?

4. What is one speaking situation in which I would like my speech to improve?

Rhythm in Sentences

Every language has its own rhythm or beat. The following figures represent two very different rhythm patterns.

If a child were dragging a stick along a picket fence with uniform slats, the rhythm pattern would be regular.

In some languages, every syllable has equal emphasis.

If another child were dragging a stick along a picket fence with slats of varying sizes and distances, the rhythm pattern would be less uniform.

In other languages, some syllables are strong and others are weak.

Which figure represents the rhythm of your language? Which figure represents the rhythm of American English?

In the previous two chapters, you learned about stressed and unstressed syllables in words. The combination of stressed and unstressed syllables helps to create the **rhythm** of English. In this chapter, you will learn about the rhythm patterns in phrases, sentences, and longer stretches of speech.

SOMETHING TO THINK ABOUT

*S*peakers of American English sometimes give full stress to every word when they are angry or adamant.

Example: *THIS PAPER WAS DUE ON MONDAY.*

If you have a tendency to stress every word and syllable equally, you might sound abrupt, angry, adamant, or impatient without intending to.

Listen!

LISTENING ACTIVITY 1

Just as words have stressed and unstressed syllables, so do phrases and sentences.

Listen to your teacher or the speaker on the tape say these word/phrase pairs. Notice that the rhythm of the short phrase is the same as the rhythm of the word in each pair.

Example: re JEC ted   He WRECKED it.

	Words	*Phrases*
1.	engineer	He was here.
2.	overthrow	In a row.
3.	himself	An elf.
4.	convert, v.	He's hurt.
5.	presented	She sent it.
6.	progressed	The best.
7.	permit, n.	Learn it.
8.	volunteer	She can hear.

LISTENING ACTIVITY 2

In each of the boxes below, there are three phrases. Each phrase has a **different** number of syllables but takes about the **same** length of time to say. Listen to your teacher or the speaker on the tape say the phrases.

⟵——— TIME ———⟶

BROAD	VIEW
BROAD	reVIEW
BROADer	reVIEW

STRONG	TASTE
STRONGer	TASTE
STRONGer	disTASTE

SLOW	TURN
SLOWly	TURN
SLOWly	reTURN

QUICK	CALL
QUICK	reCALL
QUICKly	reCALL

NEW	VICE
NEW	deVICE
NEWest	deVICE

Did you notice that some syllables were long and stretched out? Did you notice that other syllables were short and hurried?

Now say the phrases with your teacher or the speaker on tape. Tap the two strong beats in each phrase in a regular pattern on your table along with the speaker. Make the stressed syllables fall **on** the beats and the unstressed syllables fit **between** beats.

LISTENING ACTIVITY 3

Poems and rhymes are one way to acquire the rhythm patterns of a language. Listen to your teacher or the speaker on tape say these lines from popular English children's rhymes. Pay attention to the rhythm patterns, not the words. Write the number of strong beats that you hear in each line.

Three blind mice! — *3*

See how they run! — 3

They all ran after the farmer's wife, — 4

She cut off their tails with a carving knife. — 3

Did you ever see such a sight in your life — 3

As three blind mice? — 3

One, two, — 2

Buckle my shoe; — 2

Three, four, — 2

Knock at the door; — 2

Five, six, — 2

Pick up sticks; — 2

Seven, eight, — 2

Lay them straight. — 2

LISTENING ACTIVITY 4

Listen to the incomplete dialogue below. Even though more than half the words are missing, can you guess what the dialogue is about?

CUSTOMER: ____ ____ possible ____ fly ____ Los Angeles ____ Sunday?

AGENT: Yes. ____ ____ ____ couple ____ flights. One ____ ____ 9:30 ____ ____ other ____ ____ 3:15.

CUSTOMER: What ____ ____ fare ___ coach?

AGENT: _____ round-trip fare ____ $318.00 plus tax. ____ ____ want ____ make ____ reservation?

Now listen to your teacher or the speakers on tape present the **complete** dialogue. Fill in the blanks with the pieces of information that you hear.

Check your answers with your teacher. What kinds of words did you use to fill in the gaps? Were these words strong or weak in the dialogue?

LISTENING ACTIVITY 5

In this field exercise, listen to American English speakers on television, on the radio, and in informal conversations. Pay attention to **how** things are said rather than to **what** is said.

1. Listen to overall rhythm patterns. Do you hear strong beats and weak beats?

2. Do you hear any regularity in the strong beats? Do they occur at regular intervals?

3. Do you hear more regularity in radio broadcasts or in informal conversations?

4. Notice body movements and gestures, especially when a speaker says stressed words. Are mouth and jaw movements more noticeable? Is there more head movement? Are there more arm and hand gestures?

5. Notice the unstressed words. Are they hard to understand? Why? Are they necessary for understanding?

Discuss your observations with your classmates and your teacher.

Rules and Practices: Stressed and Reduced Words

Listeners of English expect certain words to be strong and other words to be weak. The strong words are the ones the listeners pay the most attention to. Sharply contrasting the strong, prominent words with the weak, obscure words is a part of clear communication.

In the *Listen!* section, you listened to stressed words and syllables and unstressed words and syllables.

What kinds of words were stressed? _____

What kinds of words were unstressed or weakened? _____

Read the guidelines that follow and see how they compare with what you wrote.

Rule 7-1

 Stress important content words like these:

Nouns	Verbs	Adjectives	Adverbs
LUNCH	VOTE	CHEAP	QUITE
ANswer	exPLAIN	ACtive	REALly

Negatives	wh-Question Words	Demonstratives
CAN'T	HOW	THIS
NOT	WHO	THOSE

Examples of stressed content words: OUR LUNCH was CHEAP.
WHY WON'T they GIVE me an ANswer?

Note: In content words of more than one syllable, just stress the appropriate syllable.

Rule 7-2

 Reduce or weaken function words. Function words serve a grammatical purpose, but don't carry meaning. Function words include the following:

Articles	Conjunctions	Prepositions	Pronouns	Auxiliary Verbs
a	and	to	her	can
the	or	of	you	have

Examples of reduced function words:

a. Contraction: JOHN's an OLD FRIEND.
                  (is)

b. Obscured Vowel: /Kn/ /yə/ SEE?
            (Can) (you)

c. Omitted Consonant: GIVE it to /əm/.
                           (him)

EXERCISE 1   In the following sentences, put a line (—) through the function words. Then put a line (—) through unstressed syllables of content words.

Say the sentences with the speaker on tape or practice with a partner. Your partner should listen carefully and write the number of strong beats in each sentence.

Example: ~~I~~ can't ~~under~~stand.   <u>2</u>

1. I can understand.   ____

2. Give me the book.   ____

3. He wants to leave.   ____

4. I did it as quickly as possible.   ____

5. He was sick.   ____

    Switch roles.

6. He's on line three.   ____

7. What's for dinner?   ____

8. You should take an airplane.   ____

9. Do you know my number?   ____

10. Can I call you back?   ____

EXERCISE 2

Say the rhymes and sentences below with your teacher or with the speaker on tape. Notice that the rhythm of each rhyme is repeated in the sentences that follow it

Rhyme A: THREE BLIND MICE
              (Please sit down.)
              (Come back soon.)
              (John can't go.)
              (Don't drive fast.)

              SEE HOW they RUN.
              (Don't use my name.)
              (John lost the disk.)
              (Tell Sue I called.)
              (That book is good.)

Rhyme B: HICKory DICKory DOCK
           (Do it according to plan.)
           (Give me a burger with cheese.)
           (Who is the man I should see?)

           The MOUSE ran UP the CLOCK.
           (I'd like to cash a check.)
           (He'd rather take the bus.)
           (I'll have her call you back.)

Rhyme C: TWINkle, TWINkle LITtle STAR,
           (Let me help you find your keys.)
           (Don't forget the bread and milk.)
           (Tell me why you don't agree.)

           HOW I WONder WHAT you ARE.
           (Find a space and park your car.)
           (Thanks a lot for all your help.)
           (Don't forget to leave a tip.)

Did you notice that you had to compress and weaken unstressed words and syllables in order to maintain the rhythm patterns?

EXERCISE 3

Say the following phrases and sentences **with** your teacher or the speaker on tape.

   Notice that phrase **a** is like a telegram and contains only a few important content words. Phrases **b**, **c**, and so on have function words added, but take the same length of time to say. Tap a pencil on the table to help you keep the rhythm.

←————————————— TIME —————————————→

1. a. FIre KItchen.

   b. FIre in KItchen.

   c. FIre in the KItchen.

   d. A FIre in the KItchen.

   e. It's a FIre in the KItchen.

2. a. SNOW exPECted FRIday.

   b. SNOW is exPECted FRIday.

   c. SNOW is exPECted on FRIday.

   d. Some SNOW is exPECted on FRIday.

3. a. DeLIver BOOKS MONday.

    b. DeLIver BOOKS by MONday.

    c. DeLIver the BOOKS by MONday.

    d. We'll deLIver the BOOKS by MONday.

    e. We'll have deLIvered the BOOKS by MONday.

How do speakers of American English weaken or compress function words? Here are some common one-syllable function words and their unstressed or reduced forms. These native speaker simplifications are **not** errors. If you compress and weaken these words, your speech will sound more natural. If you stress these words, your speech might sound monotonous.

Function Words	Unstressed Pronunciation	Examples
Articles		
a	/ə/	a mistake
the	/ðə/	on the bed
an	/ən/	an emergency
Conjunctions		
or	/ər/	pass or fail
and	/ən/ or /n/	hot and humid
Prepositions		
of	/ə/	deck of cards
	/əv/	out of eggs
to	/tə/	gone to lunch
for	/fər/	call for John
at	/ət/	at home
Pronouns		
him	/əm/ or /ɪm/	tell him
her	/ər/	introduce her
them	/əm/	warn them
you	/yə/	are you tired?
Auxiliary Verbs		
do	/də/	what do you want?
can	/kən/ or /kn/	can you go?
have	/əv/ or /ə/	must have gone

Note: Occasionally function words have stressed pronunciations.

He CAN'T SWIM, *CAN* he? (in a tag question)

He *IS* SICK. (for special emphasis)

You will learn more about special emphasis in the next chapter.

EXERCISE 4

Practice listening to unstressed function words. Fill in the blanks with the words that you hear. Note: Each sentence will have one reduced pronoun or auxiliary with a disappearing *h*, such as *h̸im, h̸er, h̸is, h̸e, h̸as,* or *h̸ave.*

Example: __Did__ __he__ get the promotion?

1. _____ _____ running in the marathon?

2. _____ _____ car be ready by this evening?

3. He's never used _____ credit cards.

4. He picked up _____ children.

5. I wish I could help _____.

6. _____ _____ _____ gotten lost?

7. The interviewer asked _____ some questions.

8. He talked about _____ travels.

9. _____ _____ had two heart attacks.

10. That's what _____ said.

EXERCISE 5

Practice blending verb endings with reduced pronouns. Say the sentences after your teacher or the speaker on tape or take turns with a partner.

Examples: confused̸ h̸im
              (confuse-dəm)   **not**   confused/him

              approached̸ h̸er
              (approach-tər)   **not**   approached/her

1. blame-dəm.   I blamed̸ h̸im for the accident.

2. check-dəm   I checked̸ them out of the library.

3. drop-tər   I dropped̸ h̸er off at eight.

4. hand-zəm   She always hands them in on time.

5. keep-sər   Her new job keeps her busy.

6. look-təm   He looked him in the eye.

7. call-dər   Her roommate called her to the phone.

8. interview-dəm   I interviewed him for a job.

9. ask-tər   He asked her for change.

10. pay-zəm   The company pays them twice a month.

***L**earners of English are frequently misunderstood when they use the words* can *and* can't.
The word can't *is stressed. It has a strong, long, clear /æ/ vowel sound.*

Example: *I CæN'T GO.*

The word can *is unstressed. It has an obscure, hurried /ə/ vowel sound (or no vowel sound at all).*

Example: *I cən GO. (or) I cn GO.*

To distinguish between can *and* can't, *English speakers rely on stress patterns, not the presence or absence of* 't.

Examples: *I can TOLerate the HEAT.*
            I CAN'T TOLerate the HEAT.

EXERCISE 6

Listen to your teacher or the speaker on the tape say the sentences below. Circle whether you heard the affirmative or negative. Check your answers with your teacher.

Then with a partner, take turns reading the sentences in the affirmative or negative. Your partner should give any response that indicates understanding.

Example: Student 1 says . . . I (can, (can't)) go to the game.

Student 2 says . . . Why not?

1. I (can, can't) call you tomorrow.

2. I (can, can't) understand this equation.

3. She (can, can't) meet with me today.

4. You (can, can't) make an appointment with me tomorrow.

5. He (can, can't) come to the party.

6. You (were, weren't) told to do that.

7. The missing books (were, weren't) found.

8. They (were, weren't) here yesterday.

9. We (are, aren't) disappointed.

10. I (can, can't) be there by nine.

Communicative Practice: Making an Appointment

Practice rhythm patterns as you work with a partner to schedule a mutually convenient business appointment.

Step 1

Preview the rhythm patterns in the sample sentences below. Pay special attention to the use of *can* and *can't*.

I can MEET on MONday at TEN.

I can MEET from TWO to THREE.

I CAN'T MEET you then. I'm GOing to the DENtist.

Can you MEET at TWELVE?

I'm BUsy from ONE to TWO.

WHAT about FRIday at TEN?

Step 2

Choose one of the following sets of roles. Decide who will play Role A and who will play Role B.

___ A. Software Consultant
   B. Client (Health Maintenance Organization)

___ A. Engineering Professor/Adviser
   B. Student Research Assistant

___ A. Factory Supervisor
   B. Vice-President of Production

___ A. Accountant
   B. Client (Restaurant Owner)

___ A. Business Professor/Lecturer
   B. Director of Training for Marketing Firm

Step 3

Write the purpose of the appointment.

_____

_____

Step 4

In the weekly schedules that follow, fill in the remaining shaded boxes with commitments typical for the role you are playing. Without looking at each other's weekly schedules, fill in Agenda A for Role A and Agenda B for Role B. Choose from the list of commitments below or create your own. Unshaded boxes should remain unscheduled. When you have completed the schedules, sit back to back, initiate the phone call, tell your partner why you want to meet, and find a suitable time when both of you are available.

LIST OF COMMITMENTS

director's meeting	client meeting
out of town	lunch with CEO
conference	Japanese language class
seminar	aerobics
staff meeting	software design

SCHEDULE/ROLE A

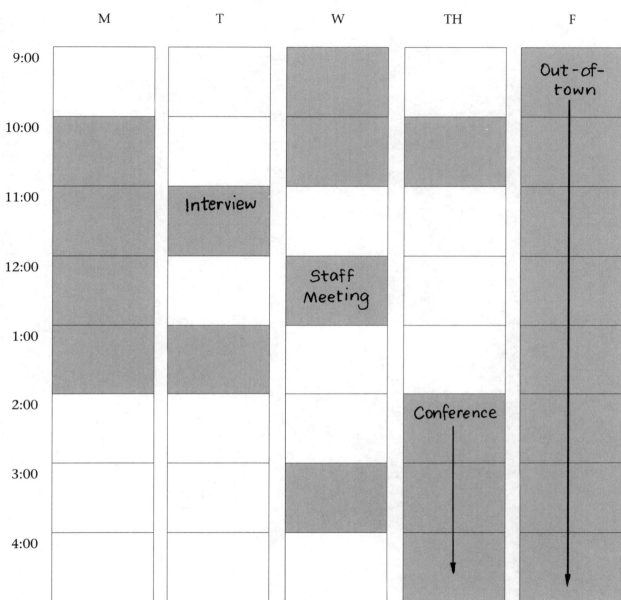

SCHEDULE/ROLE B

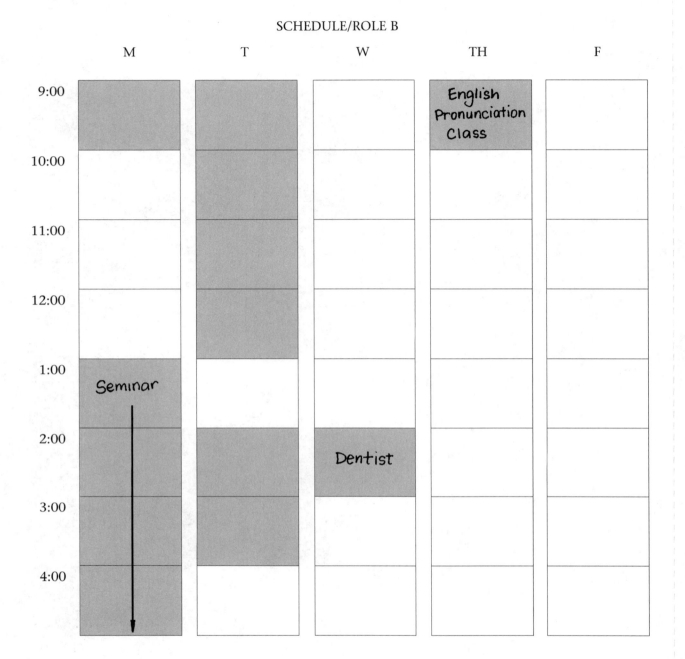

Extend Your Skills . . . to Recording a Message

You have just purchased a telephone answering machine for your home or office. Write a message to your callers in the space below. Underline the content words (or the stressed syllables of the content words). Tape record your message. Listen to the tape and evaluate your rhythm patterns. Are your stressed words and syllables longer than your unstressed words and syllables?

Message:_____

_____

_____

_____

_____

_____

_____

_____

"Could you give me a moment to collect my thoughts? It's been some time since I spoke over the phone to an actual person."

Drawing by Joe Mirachi; © 1991 *The New Yorker Magazine*, Inc. Reprinted by permission.

Oral Review: Rhythm in Sentences

Name _____

Schedule an individual consultation with your instructor, complete the review as a group project, or submit the review on tape.

Directions: Say the following famous quotations. Pay special attention to rhythm patterns. Stress and lengthen content words. Weaken and compress function words.

WORDS OF WISDOM

1. That's one small step for man, one giant leap for mankind.   —Neil Armstrong, stepping onto the surface of the moon.

2. Genius is one percent inspiration and ninety-nine percent perspiration.   —Thomas Edison

3. You are never fully dressed until you wear a smile.   —Charley Willey

4. A true friend is the best possession.   —Benjamin Franklin

5. Ask not what your country can do for you—ask what you can do for your country.   —John F. Kennedy

6. Laugh and the world laughs with you. Weep, and you weep alone. —Ella Wheeler Wilcox

7. Common sense is genius dressed in its working clothes.   —Ralph Waldo Emerson

8. I don't want to achieve immortality through my work. I want to achieve it through not dying.   —Woody Allen

9. It usually takes me more than three weeks to prepare a good impromptu speech.   —Mark Twain

10. We have nothing to fear but fear itself.   —Winston Churchill

Now add your favorite "quotable quote" or words of wisdom. If you translate from your language, communicate the meaning in English as well as you can.

11. _____

Listen to your tape before you submit it. Did you emphasize the stressed words and syllables? Did you reduce the unstressed syllables and function words?

Sentence Focus and Intonation

In Chapter 7 you learned that function words are **deemphasized** and content words are **emphasized**. However, one word in every sentence receives extra emphasis. This word is more important than the others and is called the focus word.

In written English, we indicate extra emphasis with capital letters, underlining, boldface, or italics. Here are two examples with boldface:

Just because one thing happens after another does not necessarily mean it was **caused** by it.

Some people pride themselves on how **little** they know about computers.

In spoken English, we indicate the most important word or the focus word with our voices. By giving extra emphasis to different words in a sentence, we can change the meaning.

I was a STUdent at SOUTHern TÉCH.* (not at M.I.T.)

I was a STÚdent at Southern Tech. (not a professor)

I WÁS a student at Southern Tech. (I'm no longer a student there.)

When a conversation begins or a topic is introduced, the focus word is normally the last content word. Here are examples of **normal** sentence focus.

WHERE are you GÓing?

I NEED to BORrow your CÁR.

After a conversation has begun, the focus can shift to other words to highlight important new information or to emphasize special meaning. Here are examples of **special** sentence focus.

Dialogue 1 (between passengers at the airport):

x: WHERE are you GÓing?

y: To BÓSton. WHERE are YÓU going?

*In this text, a dot (•) above a stressed word signifies sentence focus.

*Tape 2
Side B*

Dialogue 2 (between a father and son):

X: I NEED to BORrow your CAR.

Y: WHICH car?

X: Your NEW car.

In this chapter, you'll learn about normal focus words and special focus words.

*S*entence focus not only affects the meaning of a sentence. It also maintains the natural flow of communication. For example, if someone asked you . . .

WHAT did you THINK of the MEETing?

. . . and you responded with the same question,

WHAT did you THINK of the MEETing?

instead of shifting the focus from MEETing to YOU,

WHAT did YOU think of the meeting?

your colleague might think you hadn't heard the question or that you were making fun of him or her.

SOMETHING TO THINK ABOUT

Listen!

As you listen for sentence focus in this section, see whether you can discover what speakers do with their voices to call attention to focus words.

LISTENING ACTIVITY 1

Listen to this dialogue between college roommates. Put a dot (•) above the most prominent word or the focus word in each phrase or sentence. The first one has been done for you.

MIDTERM ANXIETY

X: I've got to study! Where've I put my book?

Y: Which book?

X: My calculus book.

Y: Maybe it's on the bookshelf.

X: The bookshelf is full of your comic books.

Y: Then look in the bedroom.

x: I've looked in the bedroom. I give up. This place is a mess! I can't find anything in this place.

y: Wait a minute. Your book is right there . . . in your hand.

Check your answers with your teacher.

Listen to the dialogue one more time.

LISTENING ACTIVITY 2

Listen to your teacher or the speaker on tape present this short introduction to a lecture on pollution. Put a small circle above the focus word (or the stressed syllable of the focus word) in each phrase or sentence.

"OK, today we'll continue our discussion of pollution. . . . Yesterday we defined pollution. . . . Today we'll talk about the impact of pollution . . . its far-reaching effects. Many people think pollution is just a problem for scientists . . . but it's not just a problem for scientists. It's a problem that affects everyone . . . since it affects human lives, it's a health problem . . . since it affects property, it's an economic problem . . . and since it affects our appreciation of nature, it's an aesthetic problem."

Check your answers with your teacher. What was the focus word in the first phrase? Why do you think it shifted to a different word in the next phrase?

Listen again and pay attention to rhythm patterns. What happens to the words and syllables that follow the focus word in each phrase or sentence?

LISTENING ACTIVITY 3

Listen for the *special* focus word in each statement. Check the most likely meaning.

1. Make that a medium pepperoni pizza.

    ____ Not a large.

    ____ Not a sausage.

2. I sprained my ankle playing soccer.

    ____ Not my wrist.

    ____ I didn't break it.

3. Did you fax the invoice to ATM Industries?

   ____ No, my assistant did it.

   ____ No, I mailed it.

   ____ No, just the report.

4. Change that order to a large iced tea.

   __ Rather than hot.

   __ Instead of medium.

5. Excuse me. Did you say that . . . (A + B) $\times$ C = Y?

   __ No, (A – B).

   __ No, divided by C.

Check your answers with your teacher.

How do speakers highlight the important word or the focus word in a sentence? They use a combination of **stress** and **intonation.**

Stress

The last stressed word in a sentence is the word that listeners pay the most attention to! In **normal** focus, the last stress is usually on the last content word.

I was a STUdent at SOUTHern TECH.

In **special** focus, the last stress shifts to the special focus word.

I was a STUdent at Southern Tech.

Intonation

At the end of a sentence, the intonation (or pitch) falls or rises. The word on which the pitch falls to signify statements and *wh*-questions or rises to signify yes/no questions is the word that listeners pay the most attention to! In **normal** sentence focus, the pitch falls or rises on the last content word or the stressed syllable of the last content word.

I was a STUdent at SOUTHern TECH.

WHEN did you GRADuate?

Were you a STUdent at SOUTHern TECH?

In **special** sentence focus, the pitch falls or rises on the special focus word or the stressed syllable of the special focus word.

I was a STUdent at SOUTHern TECH.

WHEN did YOU graduate?

Were you a STUdent at Southern Tech?

Note: Sometimes speakers use an extra high pitch in special focus words.

(WHEN did YOU graduate?)

Rules and Practices: Normal and Special Focus Words

Sentence focus is an important part of clear communication. It tells your listener what is important. It focuses your listener's attention on new information and draws the listener's attention away from old or less relevant information.

EXERCISE 1 Practice normal sentence focus in typical statements and questions that might begin conversations.

Listen to each sentence. Put this symbol (⌒) above each focus word with a falling intonation and this symbol (⌒) above each focus word with rising intonation.

STATEMENTS AND WH-QUESTIONS

Examples: I LOCKED my KEYS in my CAR.

WHEN do we GET our PAYchecks?

1. I need a good dictionary.

2. Where is the closest money machine?

3. I need to make an appointment with you.

4. I'm looking for a good autobiography.

5. Let's turn on the dehumidifier.

YES/NO QUESTIONS

Examples: Did you LOCK the KEYS in the CAR?

Did we GET our PAYchecks?

6. Could I borrow your dictionary?

7. Do you know where the closest money machine is?

8. Could I make an appointment with you?

9. Do you have any autobiographies?

10. Did someone turn on the dehumidifier?

Check your answers with your teacher.

Repeat the sentences or take turns saying the sentences with a partner. Use good basic rhythm patterns.

Note: If the final stress is the final syllable in the sentence, the voice glides down.

I ATE.

If the final stress is not the final syllable, the voice steps down.

I ATE it.

Rule 8-1

If information is new or just introduced, sentence focus usually shifts to the new piece of information.

Examples: "OK, we'll continue our discussion of pollution. Yesterday, we defined pollution. Today we'll talk about the impact of pollution."

x: Who is responsible for hiring?

y: Dr. Woods is responsible for hiring.

Note: The words that follow the sentence focus in each phrase or sentence are backgrounded.

EXERCISE 2

Practice special sentence focus to highlight new information and to background old information. Say the dialogues **with** the speakers on tape or practice them with a partner.

Example: x: I need some shrimp.

y: How much shrimp?

x: A pound.

DIALOGUE 1

x: When's the party?

y: Which party?

x: The staff party.

y: It's Tuesday night.

x: But there's a meeting on Tuesday night.

y: What kind of meeting?

x: A curriculum meeting.

y: No. That's been postponed.

DIALOGUE 2

x: Who gave the presentation?

y: Paul gave it.

x: Did he write it?

y: No, Frank wrote it.

EXERCISE 3

Listen to the questions below. Answer the questions by highlighting a different word in each answer. Check your responses with your teacher or with the model on tape.

1. Who gave Dave a present?

Terry gave Dave a present.

2. Who did Terry give a present to?

Terry gave Dave a present.

3. What did Terry give Dave?

Terry gave Dave a present.

Rule 8-2

✓ Use special sentence focus to emphasize contrasts.

Example: Change that order to a large iced tea. (*Large* contrasts with the size of iced tea previously ordered.)

EXERCISE 4

Practice special sentence focus for contrast. Say the sentences, comparing your productions to those of the speaker on the tape. Or practice with a partner, monitoring for sentence focus.

1. This isn't the twenty-fifth floor; it's the twenty-sixth floor.

2. He found his wallet, but he didn't find his credit cards.

3. Excuse me. I'd like to move from the smoking section to the nonsmoking section.

4. I made the check out to John Keenan instead of Joan Keenan.

5. I thought his birthday was on the fourteenth, but it's on the fifteenth.

Rule 8-3

✓ Use sentence focus to correct, contradict, or modify an earlier statement.

Example: X: Class will be over at four-thirty.

   Y: Oh. I thought class would be over at five-thirty.

EXERCISE 5

Modify the following incorrect statements, using special sentence focus to highlight the corrected element. Practice your corrected statements with a partner. Monitor your partner. Try to incorporate these expressions:

Are you sure?   I thought . . .   I always thought . . .

Actually, . . .   I'm not sure that's right . . .

I was under the impression . . .   I don't think so . . .

As a matter of fact, . . .

Example: INCORRECT: In Japanese management practice, individuals make decisions.

   CORRECT: I was under the impression that . . . groups make decisions.

1. The Third World refers to countries that are economically developed.

2. A mainframe computer is commonly found in the home.

3. A tachometer measures earthquake activity.

4. Philosophy is the study of personality.

5. The Amazon River is the longest river in the world.

6. K is the chemical symbol for gold.

7. Washington, D.C., is the headquarters for the U.N.

8. Mt. Kilimanjaro is usually considered to be the highest mountain in the world.

9. The Berlin Wall was built to stop the flow of refugees from West Germany to East Germany.

10. Computer hardware includes computer programs.

Rule 8-4

☑ Use sentence focus to emphasize agreement.

Example: x: This chapter's easy.

   y: You're right. It is easy.

Note: In the case of special sentence focus, we sometimes make an exception to basic rhythm by stressing function words. For example, when emphasizing agreement, we stress the verb *to be,* the auxiliary, or *do, does,* or *did.*

EXERCISE 6 Practice using sentence focus to emphasize agreement. Work with a partner.

Student 1 fills in the blank with something that is true and then says the sentence. Student 2 uses sentence focus to agree with everything Speaker 1 says. Switch roles and repeat the exercise.

Example: STUDENT 1: ___**Frank**___ studies hard.

   STUDENT 2: He does study hard. (or) He does.

1. _____ is a great singer.

2. _____ serves terrific ethnic food.

3. _____ is a beautiful city.

4. _____ is the best car on the road.

5. _____ was a wonderful movie.

*When a piece of information is **especially** important, there are several ways, in addition to special sentence focus, to draw a listener's attention to it. To highlight an important word or a key term:*

1. *Say it slowly.*

2. *Say it softly.*

3. *Repeat it.*

4. *Paraphrase it.*

5. *Emphasize it with a hand or arm gesture or a head nod.*

6. *Use an introductory transition phrase (e.g., The point is . . . ; The bottom line is . . . ; The crucial point is . . .).*

In the next exercise, you will practice using gestures.

Communicative Practice: Making Inferences

Use sentence focus to make inferences. Imagine that you have just entered a room in the middle of a discussion or a meeting, and you hear one of the statements below. With a partner, create a statement that might have **preceded** the one you hear.

Practice saying the "preceding statements" and "statements" with your partner. In the "statements," use an arm gesture, a hand gesture, or a head nod to give added emphasis to the focus words.

Be prepared to present selected dialogues to your class.

Example: Preceding Statement: **This plan has a lot of advantages.**

Statement: Actually, John, I think the plan has a lot of DISadvantages.

1. Preceding Statement: _____
   Statement: Let's put in an order for TWO new PCs.

2. Preceding Statement: _____
   Statement: These plans are NOT affordable. Have the architect make some modifications.

3. Preceding Statement: _____
   Statement: I went to the lab on Saturday AND Sunday.

4. Preceding Statement: _____
   Statement: That IS an unrealistic deadline.

5. Preceding Statement: _____
   Statement: Iris, could YOU do the presentation on marketing techniques?

6. Preceding Statement: _____

   Statement: I was told the dress would be INformal.

7. Preceding Statement: _____

   Statement: No, it isn't.   The final exam is on the FIFTH of December.

8. Preceding Statement: _____

   Statement: What about the LONG-term effects?

9. Preceding Statement: _____

   Statement: Well, then, how about if everyone chips in FIVE dollars?

10. Preceding Statement: _____

    Statement: Well then, how much would it cost to RENT a copy machine?

Extend Your Skills . . . to a Contrastive Analysis

When you are speaking, you need to compare and contrast many times a day at home, at work, and at school. You might need to weigh the merits of one university over another, the purchase of one piece of equipment over another, or the choice of one vacation spot over another.

CONTRASTIVE ANALYSIS ACTIVITY: The Japanese style of management has become a source of interest to people all over the world. In the book *With Respect to the Japanese,* author John Condon outlines the differences between the U.S. and Japanese styles of communication and management. This information is presented below.

Student 1 has information about the Japanese managerial style. Student 2 has information about the American managerial style. Practice sentence focus as you complete your outlines.

Step 1

Preview key vocabulary. Review sound/spelling and stress patterns.

self-identification	mobility
personal relations	ability
valued qualities	immediate future
future orientation	business associates
social time	family obligations
specialists	communication
decision-making	

Step 2

Get the information that you need to complete your outline from your partner. Share information verbally; do not look at each other's charts. Use sentence focus to highlight contrasting elements.

Example: STUDENT 1: In Japan, there's generally low upward mobility.

STUDENT 2: Well, in the United States, there's high upward mobility.

Step 3

If there are students from Japan in your class, ask them if there are any points in the outline that they disagree with. With your class, discuss the differences that are the most important when doing business internationally.

Step 4

In groups of four to six students, compare and contrast the business/work customs of the countries represented in your group in the following areas:

a. business cards

b. handshakes

c. gift giving

d. dress codes

e. length of a typical workday

f. length of a typical workweek

g. length of annual vacation

JAPAN		
Area	*Japanese Pattern*	*U.S. Pattern*
Self-Identification	Always part of a group	
Valued Qualities	Character and trust; generalists valued	
Promotion	Low upward mobility	
Job Mobility	Low job mobility; life-long employment is common	
Communication	Indirect; vagueness helps avoid conflict; listening and reading valued over public speaking	
Decision Making	Bottom-up; relatively slow; consensus is sought; conflict is avoided	
Loyalty	Loyalty to organization takes precedence over immediate family obligations	
Time	Promptness is valued; time is divided between formal work time and informal social time with business associates	
Future Orientation	Conscious of long-term future; concern for long-range planning	

Charts adapted from John C. Condon, "Communication and Management Styles," in *With Respect to the Japanese* (Yarmouth, Me.: Intercultural Press, 1984), pp. 64–66. Reprinted with permission.

UNITED STATES		
Area	*Japanese Pattern*	*U.S. Pattern*
Self-Identification		Primarily an individual; secondarily, part of a group
Valued Qualities		Ability; specialists valued
Promotion		High upward mobility
Job Mobility		High job mobility
Communication		Direct and explicit; vagueness may be irritating; speaking ability valued over listening and reading
Decision Making		Top-down; relatively fast; consensus desirable but not sought; conflict is expected
Loyalty		Immediate family obligations may take precedence over loyalty to organization
Time		Promptness is valued; time is divided between work and private (personal and family) time
Future Orientation		Conscious of immediate future; more concern for short-range planning

Oral Review: Sentence Focus and Intonation

Name_____

Schedule an individual consultation with your teacher, complete the review as a pair project, or submit the review on tape.

Part A

Review normal sentence focus. Say these sentences as if you were beginning a conversation or introducing a topic.

Example: The typical workday in the United States is eight hours.

1. Mr. Lee speaks three languages fluently.

2. Did you schedule an appointment with me at five on Friday?

3. He has a master's degree in industrial engineering.

4. Jim is talking with his ex-wife.

5. John received a research assistantship.

Listen to the sentences. Did you use good basic rhythm patterns?

Part B

Review special sentence focus. Say each sentence two times. Each time, make the word with the circled letter above it the special focus word. (The meanings are given in parentheses.) Or review with a partner as follows.

Say one of the sentences in each pair. Your partner should give the correct meaning/response in parentheses.

Example: a. The typical workday in the United States is eight hours.

(Not in Mexico or Japan.)

b. The typical workday in the United States is eight hours.
(Not ten hours.)

1. a. Mr. Lee speaks three languages fluently.

(Not two.)

b. Mr. Lee speaks three languages fluently.

(Not Mrs. Lee.)

2.   a. Did you schedule an appointment with me at 5:00 Ⓐ on Friday?

        (That's right. At five.)

    b. Did you schedule an appointment with me at 5:00 Ⓑ on Friday?

        (No, with Dr. Bell.)

3.   a. He has a master's Ⓐ degree in industrial engineering.

        (Not a doctorate.)

    b. He has a master's degree in industrial Ⓑ engineering.

        (Not in civil engineering.)

4.   a. Jim is talking to his ex-Ⓐ wife.

        (Didn't you know he'd been married before?)

    b. Jim is Ⓑ talking to his ex-wife.

        (Not arguing.)

5.   a. John received a research Ⓐ assistantship.

        (Not a teaching assistantship.)

    b. Ⓑ John received a research assistantship.

        (Not Joan.)

    Listen to the sentences. Did you highlight the focus words? Make corrections at the end of your tape.

More Functions of Intonation

FOX TROT   by Bill Amend

Fox Trot © 1988, Universal Press Syndicate

Intonation is the rise and fall in the pitch of the voice. In Chapter 8, you learned how rising and falling intonation signals the focus words in statements and questions.

In this chapter, you will learn about intonation to present choices, list items in a series, request clarification, address people by name, and indicate surprise.

You'll learn how intonation can change a statement . . .

He's CLOSing his CHECKing account. ⟶

to a question

He's CLOSing his CHECKing account? ⟶

You'll learn how intonation can change a simple information question . . .

WHO are you MARrying?

to a request for clarification.

WHO are you marrying?

You'll also learn how it can transform a yes/no question . . .

Would you LIKE SOMEthing to EAT or DRINK?

into a question in which you are presenting a choice.

Would you LIKE SOMEthing to EAT or DRINK?

Listen!

LISTENING ACTIVITY

What are the intonation or pitch patterns in the following sentences? Listen to the speaker on tape or ask a native English speaker to say the sentences and listen carefully. Draw a rising arrow ⤴ or falling arrow ⤵ over the stressed words (or syllables) with a significant pitch rise or pitch fall. Some of the sentences may have two or more arrows.

Example: We'll have to take either a taxi or a bus.

1. It's time to eat, Ms. Baker.

2. This is a good place to park, Dr. Sitter.

3. Would you rather live in a condominium or an apartment?

4. Sometimes I don't know whether I'm coming or going.

5. She's going to study physics, mathematics, or chemistry.

6. Intonation patterns can convey emotions like surprise, annoyance, excitement, and disappointment.

7. Is this form due this week or next week?

8. x: What time is your plane?

   y: What time?

9. x: The number is 252-8764.

   y: 252-8764?

10. Should we leave a tip of 15% or 20%?

Compare your findings with those of the other members of the class.

Rules and Practices

Some intonation patterns express attitudes and emotions like anger, doubt, irony, and sarcasm. These patterns are variable and difficult to learn. Other intonation patterns are essential for giving information and participating in discussions and conversations.

Rule 9-1

Listen to this example of a sentence that presents a choice. How do you know a choice is being offered?

Example: Is the exam today or tomorrow?

In a statement or a question that involves a choice between two alternatives, indicate the first choice with a rising pitch on the stressed syllable of the first item; indicate the second choice with a falling pitch on the stressed syllable of the second item.

Example: We can meet in your office or mine.

EXERCISE 1

Say these sentences **with** your teacher or the speaker on tape. Add three sentences that present choices of your own. Then with a partner take turns saying all the sentences.

1. Is the light green or red?
2. The maximum speed limit is either 55 or 65.
3. You should walk on the sidewalk or on the shoulder.
4. Did you get a new car or a used car?
5. Signal a turn with your blinker or your arm.
6. Should I turn left or right?
7. Do you want to walk or ride?
8.
9.
10.

Rule 9-2

Listen to the example of a sentence with two or more items in a list. How do you know there are more items on the list? How do you know when the speaker has reached the last item?

Example: In one day, I lost my keys, my wallet, and my plane ticket.

☑ When you are presenting two or more items in a series, the pitch rises on the stressed syllable of every item except the last. The rising pitch tells your listener there is more to come. The pitch falls on the stressed syllable of the last item. The falling pitch tells your listener you have reached the end of the series.

Example: While you're at the store, get some dog food, coffee filters,

and chicken breasts.

EXERCISE 2   With a partner, fill in the blanks in each series of items. Take turns saying the sentences. Monitor your partner's intonation.

1. The EPA (Environmental Protection Agency) protects the air, soil, and _____.

2. If I get a PC, I'll need a table, a printer, and a _____.

3. Grades are often based on class participation, projects, and _____ _____.

4. The fringe benefits include two weeks of paid vacation every year, one day of paid sick leave every month, and _____.

5. Is it easier for you to read, write, or _____in English?

EXERCISE 3   Items in a series can be words, phrases, or even clauses. Choose one of the situations below and create a response. Then give your response orally to the class or to a small group of four to six.

    a. You are employed by an engineering firm. You are preparing to give a technical presentation on heat transfer to some clients who don't have technical backgrounds. There are three ways heat energy can be transferred from one place to another: conduction, convection, and radiation. You plan to explain all three in your presentation. Give a short, interesting introduction to your talk and introduce the three methods of heat transfer.

Introduction with the three major subtopics:

_____

_____

_____

_____

b. It is Saturday afternoon. Your twelve-year-old son wants you to take him and his friends to a movie this afternoon. However, he not only failed to do his chores for the week (taking out the garbage, feeding the dog, bundling the newspaper, and cutting the grass), but he also fought with his brother all week and his room is a mess. Respond to your son's request and give him three good reasons why he shouldn't go to the movies.

Three good reasons:

_____

_____

_____

c. You have been working diligently on a report for your supervisor for the past two weeks. The deadline is today, but, due to circumstances beyond your control, the report is not ready. The office computers were down for three days last week, someone who has vital information has been out of town all week, your uncle died last week and you had to attend the funeral, and the deadline was unrealistic in the first place. In a diplomatic way, ask your boss for an extension and give him or her three good reasons why the extension is justified.

Three good reasons:

_____

_____

_____

Rule 9-3

In this example, how does speaker Y indicate surprise?

X: He has ten brothers.

Y: He has ten brothers? (I'm really surprised.)

You can show surprise or disbelief by echoing a statement using rising pitch. The pitch rise is usually on the stressed syllable of the last content word.

X: She's a grandmother.

Y: She's a grandmother? (You're kidding. She looks so young.)

Rule 9-4

Listen to the pattern for requesting clarification or more information. It is the same as the pattern for surprise.

✓ If you want clarification of the entire statement the pitch rises on the last content word.

x: I broke my leg.

y: You broke your leg? (How did you do that?)

If you want clarification of a specific item, the focus shifts and the pitch rises on the specific item you want clarified.

x: The number is 367-2435.

y: 367-2435? (The speaker wants clarification of the third number.)

EXERCISE 4

Say the following dialogues **with** the speakers on tape or practice them with a partner. Speaker Y should show surprise or disbelief and incorporate one of these introductory expressions:

You're kidding . . .	You're joking . . .
You've got to be kidding . . .	No way . . .
I don't believe it . . .	You can't be serious . . .

Example: x: John lost his job.
        y: You're kidding . . . he lost his job?

1. x: He's majoring in economics.

   y: He's majoring in economics? He can't even balance his checkbook.

2. x: I failed statistics.

   y: You failed statistics?

3. x: I'm moving to the Pacific Northwest.

   y: You're moving to the Pacific Northwest? Why?

4. x: Carl totaled his car.

   y: He totaled his car? Was he hurt?

5. x: The cheapest round-trip fare is 1,500 dollars.

   y: The cheapest fare is 1,500 dollars?

Rule 9-5

Listen to these two dialogues. Why did speaker X answer the same question in two different ways?

Dialogue 1:   X: I'm going to the Middle East.

     Y: Where?

     X: Lebanon.

Dialogue 2:   X: I'm going to the Middle East.

     Y: Where?

     X: The Middle East.

✓ If a *wh*-question has the typical falling pitch pattern, the speaker is probably seeking information. If the *wh*-question has rising pitch, the speaker is probably requesting repetition or clarification. When seeking clarification, the pitch rise occurs on the *wh*-word.

EXERCISE 5 In this practice, Student 1 makes a statement. Student 2 responds with a *wh*-question with a rising pitch (to request repetition). Student 1 then answers. Switch roles and repeat the exercise.

Example: STUDENT 1 (X): I'm going to Brazil.

     STUDENT 2 (Y): Where are you going? or Where?

     STUDENT 1 (X): Brazil.

1. X: They moved their headquarters near campus.

 Y: Where did they move? or Where?

 X: Near campus.

2. X: I left it on the bus.

 Y: Where did you leave it? or Where?

 X: On the bus.

3. X: The next home game is this weekend.

 Y: When is it? or When?

 X: This weekend.

4. X: I'll call you in the morning.

 Y: When will you call? or When?

 X: In the morning.

5. X: Hurricane Hugo came ashore in South Carolina.

 Y: Where did it come ashore? or Where?

 X: In South Carolina.

Rule 9-6

Listen to these examples of direct address.

Examples: They've already left, Mr. Johnson.
Did they leave, Mr. Johnson?

☑ When you use direct address at the end of a sentence, a person's name is usually spoken as a separate phrase that starts low and rises only slightly.

Example: What did you buy, Mary?

EXERCISE 6

Listen as your teacher or the speaker on the tape reads sentence a or b. Circle the one you hear.

Example: a. Are you bathing children? (One focus word; children are being spoken **about**)

b. Are you bathing, children? (Two focus words; children are being spoken **to**)

1. a. We have to pay John.

    b. We have to pay, John.

2. a. We don't know Dr. White.

    b. We don't know, Dr. White.

3. a. Are you hiring Jane?

    b. Are you hiring, Jane?

4. a. We need to see Ms. Miller.

    b. We need to see, Ms. Miller.

5. a. I didn't call Lee.

    b. I didn't call, Lee.

Check your answers with your teacher. With a partner, practice saying the circled sentences. Write three sentences with direct address at the end. Use the names of people you know and use titles if appropriate. Dictate your sentences to your partner.

1. _____

2. _____

3. _____

EXERCISE 7

With a partner, mark the following dialogue for sentence focus and for rising and falling pitch patterns.

Practice the dialogue with the speakers on tape or in groups of three. Switch roles and practice it again.

ORDERING BEVERAGES

WAITER: What would you like to drink, sir?

PATRON A: Just water.

WAITER: And what would you like to drink?

PATRON B: I'll have tea.

WAITER: Hot or iced?

PATRON B: Iced.

WAITER: Sweetened or unsweetened?

PATRON B: Uh . . . unsweetened.

WAITER: Do you want that now or with your meal?

PATRON B: You can bring it now.

Communicative Practice: Impromptu Dialogues

You and your partner will be assigned to develop dialogue for one of the five situations below. Student 1 should read Role X and Student 2 should read Role Y for the same situation. Without looking at each other's role descriptions, create an impromptu dialogue beginning with Role X. Practice your dialogue until it is smooth and natural. Present it to the class.

ROLE X

SITUATION 1: Driving on a city street

ROLE X: A driver

You are driving down an uncrowded four-lane city street. You are thinking about work or school and not paying much attention to your driving. A policeman behind you signals you to pull over. You have no idea what the offense was. You are nervous, but polite. When you learned what you did, you are very apologetic.

SITUATION 2: Getting a carpet cleaned

ROLE X: An office manager

The carpet in your office suite needs to be cleaned. You have three rooms, approximately 10' × 12' to be cleaned. You find a company in the yellow pages and call for an estimate. You also ask for some references because you have never heard of the company before.

SITUATION 3: Making copies of a report

ROLE X: An employee of a company

You just completed a 150-page report for your company. Your supervisor wants 10 bound copies for a meeting at 9:00 tomorrow morning. You call a copy service to get a price and time of completion. You want white 70-lb. paper, a cover on blue 80-lb. paper, spiral binding, and text on both sides of each sheet of paper.

SITUATION 4: A supermarket mix-up

ROLE X: A customer

You have just arrived home from the supermarket. You can't find four pounds of chicken wings that you are certain you purchased. Your receipt indicates that you paid for them. You are irate because you will probably have to drive back to get them. You call the store to find out what you should do.

SITUATION 5: Complaining to an airline company

ROLE X: A passenger

You and your family have just returned to Miami from a two-week vacation on the west coast. During the five-hour Saturday morning flight from San Francisco, a movie with an extreme amount of violence was shown in the coach section. Even though you didn't rent headphones, it was hard for you to ignore the screen. You suspect the movie was rated R and feel the film was inappropriate for the many children on board. You call the airline to complain and to request the airline's criteria for selecting in-flight movies.

ROLE Y

SITUATION 1: Driving on a city street

ROLE Y: A police officer

You have just stopped a driver who entered an intersection after the light turned yellow. You request the driver's license and registration. You may or may not issue a ticket depending upon whether the driver knows it is illegal to enter an intersection on a yellow light and whether the driver seems genuinely sorry.

SITUATION 2: Getting a carpet cleaned

ROLE Y: Owner of Steam Clean Carpet Company

You give phone estimates based on room size. Cleaning the carpet in an average 125-square-foot room costs $15.95. You are currently running a grand-opening special because your company has just opened. You are offering to clean three average-sized rooms for $39.95.

SITUATION 3: Copying a company report

ROLE Y: An employee at a 24-hour copy service

Ten spiral-bound copies of the caller's report would run about $150.00. If the original were delivered within the next hour, the copies could be ready by 9:00 tonight.

SITUATION 4: A supermarket mix-up

ROLE Y: A supermarket manager

You look for the caller's purchase at all the check-outs. The chicken wings are nowhere to be seen. You guess that a cashier accidentally put them in someone else's bag. You tell the caller if he or she brings in the receipt, the store will replace the wings. However, you can sense that the customer is annoyed about the mistake, so you offer to refund the customer's money and give him or her the wings free of charge.

SITUATION 5: Complaining to an airline company

ROLE Y: Customer service employee for a major airline

Your airline company selects in-flight movies that will appeal to the majority of its customers, most of whom are male passengers traveling on business. The movie in question was rated PG-13. You don't have time to talk to this customer and you advise the caller to make a formal complaint in writing.

Extend Your Skills . . . to Surveys and Interviews

SIMULATION: In Chapter 3, you recorded a public service broadcast about environmental problems. In this simulation, you will determine the two most effective environmental solutions.

You are a member of a nonprofit environmental organization. One of your functions is to lobby or persuade local, state, and federal government to consider legislation to protect the environment.

This is the first meeting of the year. At this meeting you will choose the top two environmental solutions to which you will devote most of your limited financial and human resources.

Step 1

Preview the sound/spelling and stress patterns in the key words that are italicized in the list of solutions below.

LIST OF ENVIRONMENTAL SOLUTIONS

- Institute **tax** incentives for **insulating** or installing solar heat and **alternate** forms of heating and cooling.

- Create limited **access interstate** lanes solely for **carpools** (cars with more than one passenger).

- **Ration** gasoline.

- Lower **speed limits.**

- Restrict use of **air conditioners** to the hottest hours of the day.

- Ban aerosol sprays.

- Increase cost of garbage pickup and include **pickup** of recyclable materials (**newspaper,** glass **separated** by color, **computer paper,** aluminum, and **motor oil**).

- Ban **throwaway** beverage containers; require the purchase of returnable glass bottles.

- Restrict removal of trees for development purposes.

- Institute heavy penalties for styrofoam manufacturers.

- Increase fines for **industrial pollution.**

- Prohibit **residential** and **commercial** development near streams, rivers, and other bodies of water.

- Require annual auto **emission** inspection.

- Use pesticides sparingly.

OTHERS:

- _____

- _____

Step 2

In groups of four to six students, discuss the solutions above and add some of your own. Agree on a preliminary list of the most effective solutions.

Step 3

With your group, design a questionnaire that will give you a sampling of public opinion on environmental solutions. Relate most of your questions to solutions your committee is considering. Your questionnaire should have at least ten questions of various kinds. Practice the intonation patterns in your questions.

Preview the intonation in these sample questions:

OPEN-ENDED QUESTION

_Wh_-Question: In your opinion, what are some of the most immediate environmental threats?

CLOSED QUESTIONS

Choice Question: Would you rather pay for curbside recycling or take your materials to a recycling center?

Yes/No Question: Would you support a bill to eliminate all plastic beverage containers in the state?

ENVIRONMENTAL SOLUTIONS QUESTIONNAIRE

1.

2.

3.

4.

5.

6.

7.

8.

9.

10.

Step 4

Give your survey orally to as many people as possible. Ask follow-up questions to get clarification and more detailed responses.

Preview intonation for this sample follow-up question:

Interviewee's statement: I'm completely against gas rationing.

Interviewer's follow-up: You're against gas rationing? (Clarify/Tell me more.)

Step 5

Discuss the results of your survey with the rest of your group. Try to reach a consensus on the top two solutions.

Solution 1:_____

Solution 2:_____

Step 6

Select a spokesperson to submit your group's recommendations to the class.

Oral Review: More Functions of Intonation

Name_____

Schedule an individual consultation with your teacher, complete the review as a group project, or submit the review on tape.

Part A

Read the following short dialogues with a partner.

1. x: What was your major, Ali?

   y: Do you mean graduate or undergraduate?

2. x: Where are you going, Maria?

   y: I'm going to the bank, the dentist, and the mall.

3. x: How many people did you invite, Sandra?

   y: Fifty.

   x: How many?

   y: Fifty.

Part B

Refer to the Environmental Solutions Activity in this chapter. In **your** opinion, what are the three most effective environmental solutions? Present them in the form of a list and use intonation for items in a series.

Listen to your tape before you submit it. Make any corrections at the end of the tape.

Phrasing, Pausing, and Blending

Speakers of American English organize words into short meaningful phrases called thought groups. If a speaker doesn't divide the stream of speech into thought groups, the language might be difficult to understand, no matter how clearly pronounced each word is.

Languages signal thought groups in different ways. In American English, speakers use falling intonation or a slight drop in pitch to mark the end of a thought group. The drop in pitch is sometimes accompanied by a brief pause.

The information below is organized into thought groups to make it easier to comprehend. The end of each thought group is marked with a slash (/).

Phone number: 555/1212

Social Security Number: 360/42/5548

Sentence: In terms of male life expectancy,/ the country of Iceland/ ranks the highest/ with 74 years.

Within phrases or thought groups, English speakers make a smooth connection between words by blending or linking the final sound of one word with the beginning sound of the next word. As a result, words within thought groups often sound like one long word. It is sometimes difficult to hear where one word ends and the next word begins.

Notice the smooth transition between words in these very short sentences.

This_is_easy.

I'll_leave_a_tip.

In this chapter, you'll practice delivering information in meaningful thought groups and making a smooth transition between words in thought groups.

Listen!

LISTENING ACTIVITY 1

Listen to your teacher or the speaker on the tape say the phrases. If you hear one thought group, circle *a*. If you hear two thought groups, circle *b*.

1. a. twenty-seven-foot basketball players

   b. twenty / seven-foot basketball players

2. a. forty-eight-foot boards

   b. forty / eight-foot boards

3. a. twenty-nine-cent stamps

   b. twenty / nine-cent stamps

4. a. eighty-five-foot women

   b. eighty / five-foot women

5. a. seven-week-long vacations

   b. seven / week-long vacations

6. a. three-hour-long tests

   b. three / hour-long tests

Check your answers with your teacher. With your class, discuss how thought groups change the meanings of the phrases in the pairs above.

LISTENING ACTIVITY 2

Listen to your teacher or the speaker on tape read this transcript of a radio advertisement two times. The first time, listen for meaning. The second time, indicate the slight pitch fall marking the end of each thought group with a slash (/).

"Unlike other copier companies, Mita doesn't make cameras, or televisions, or calculators, or video cassette recorders, or bicycles, or telephone answering machines, or car stereos, or vacuum cleaners, or movies, watches, scotch recording tape, batteries or film. The fact is, Mita doesn't make anything but great copiers. After all, we didn't get to be the fastest growing copier company for the last five years by selling microwave ovens. Mita. All we make are great copiers."

Compare your answers with those of the rest of the class. What was the average number of words in the thought groups?

LISTENING ACTIVITY 3

Listen to the difference between the slight pitch fall at the end of thought groups and the deeper pitch fall at the end of statements. Your teacher or the speakers on the tape will say the statements and responses below. Circle response *a* if the speaker seems to be finished. Circle response *b* if the speaker seems to have more to say.

1. Could you give me your credit card number please?

   a. 4307/3198/4010

   b. 4307/3198/4010 . . . (8238)

2. Did you register for biology?

   a. No. I registered for chemistry.

   b. No. I registered for chemistry . . . (because . . .)

3. Can I keep the book until Monday?

   a. No. I need it this weekend.

   b. No. I need it this weekend . . . (since . . .)

4. Have you done your homework?

   a. No. I haven't done it.

   b. No. I haven't done it . . . (but . . .)

5. The copier isn't working, is it?

   a. No. It broke this morning.

   b. No. It broke this morning . . . (however, . . .)

Rules and Practices 1: Phrases and Thought Groups

Writers make ideas clear to readers by using commas, periods, and indented paragraphs. Speakers make ideas clear to listeners by using thought groups.

Decisions about where thought groups begin and end vary from speaker to speaker and from situation to situation. However, here are some general guidelines to help you communicate your thoughts more clearly.

Rule 10-1

☑ The end of a clause is often the end of a thought group. Use a slight drop in pitch and sometimes a brief pause.

Examples: Mary's away from her desk,/ but she'll be back soon.

Whatever you do,/ do well.

The phone always rings,/ when I'm in the shower.

John,/ who's my youngest brother,/ is a commercial pilot.

Notice that the slight pitch fall occurs on the stressed syllable of the last content word in each thought group.

Rule 10-2

☑ The end of a phrase is often the end of a thought group. Use a slight drop in pitch and occasionally a brief pause. Depending upon the length of the phrase, typical thought groups might include prepositional phrases, verb phrases, noun phrases, verb + object phrases, subject + verb, and subject + verb + object.

Examples: I leave for work/ at seven a.m./ every morning.

Many of the students/ want to live/ with English speakers.

Notice again that the slight pitch fall is on the stressed syllable of the last content word of each thought group (unless there is reason to shift the focus of the thought group to another word).

Rule 10-3

☑ Notice how transitional or parenthetical expressions (first, finally, of course, on the other hand) form thought groups.

Example: Our profit margin,/ as you all know, / has decreased substantially/ this past quarter.

EXERCISE 1 In small groups of three or four, unscramble the job descriptions and organize the phrases into logical sentences.

Take turns saying the sentences with the members of your group. Incorporate a slight pitch fall on the **last stressed word** (or syllable) of each thought group or the **focus** of each thought group.

Do either Section A or Section B and go on to the other section if you finish the first.

Example: 1. Professional philosophers/ are employed almost exclusively/ by colleges/ and universities.

Note: Some speakers might add a slight pitch fall after *employed;* others might omit the slight pitch fall after *colleges.*

NOUN PHRASES	VERB PHRASES	PREPOSITIONAL PHRASES
Section A:		
1. Professional philosophers	risk bodily injury	by colleges and universities
2. Most firefighters	advise clients	in their calculations
3. NFL players	must be accurate	about their hair
4. Nuclear engineers	usually travel	by fire and smoke
5. Licensed cosmetologists	are employed almost exclusively	on chartered jets
Section B:		
6. School principals	are occasionally invited	with rude and demanding people
7. Travel agents	must express their thoughts	at all times of the day and night
8. Writers of books	are on call	in group practices
9. Some secretaries	work together	in a precise manner
10. Nuclear plant decontamination experts	are forced to interact	on promotional cruises
11. A large majority of doctors	are constantly dealing	with disciplinary problems

EXERCISE 2 In each sentence, a clause or phrase has been misplaced. Put parentheses around the misplaced phrase and indicate its correct position in the sentence with a ∧. Mark the sentences for thought groups.

Say the corrected sentences with the speaker on tape or take turns saying them with a partner. Monitor for thought groups and good basic rhythm patterns.

Example: The hostess served the dinner ∧ to her guests (that she had been warming in the oven.)

1. Please take time to look over the brochure that is enclosed with your family.

2. A calf was born to a farmer with two heads.

3. Yoko Ono will talk about her husband, John Lennon, who was killed in an interview with Barbara Walters.

4. The Toyota hit a utility pole going about 45 miles per hour.

5. The patient was referred to a psychiatrist with a severe emotional problem.

6. She died in the home in which she was born at the age of 88.

7. Breaking into the window of the girl's dorm, the dean of men surprised ten members of the football team.

8. Here are some suggestions for handling obscene phone calls from the New England Telephone Company.

9. Some sources said shortly after his death Mao Tse-Tung had expressed a wish that his body be cremated.

10. Plunging 1,000 feet into the gorge, we saw Yosemite Falls.*

EXERCISE 3   The following excerpt is from an August 1969 interview with the Apollo 11 astronauts, Collins, Aldrin, and Armstrong, after their flight to the moon.

Imagine packaging each of the very long sentences into several small bundles or thought groups. Mark the sentences with a slash (/) for thought groups.

With a partner, compare your thought groups. Practice the question/answer exchange and then record it.

REPORTER: I'm struck from the movies and the still pictures by the difference in the very hostile appearance of the moon when you're orbiting over it or some distance from it and the warmer colors and the relatively apparently more friendly appearance of it when you're on the surface. I'd like to ask Colonel Collins if he gets that same impression from the pictures and the two of you who were on the moon, what impression do you have along those lines?

---

*From Richard Lederer, *Anguished English* (New York: Laurel, 1987), pp. 150–154. Copyright Wyrick & Company. Reprinted by permission.

Collins: The moon changes character as the angle of the sunlight strik-
ing its surface changes. At very low sun angles close to the termina-
tor at dawn or dusk, it has the harsh, forbidding characteristics
which you see in a lot of the photographs. On the other hand, when
the sun is more closely overhead, the midday situation, the moon
takes on more of a brown color. It becomes almost a rosy looking
place—a fairly friendly place so that from dawn through midday
through dusk you run the whole gamut. It starts off very forbidding,
becomes friendly, and then becomes forbidding again as the sun dis-
appears.*

Listen to your recording. Do you hear clearly marked thought
groups? Do you hear good basic rhythm patterns (stressed and reduced
words) within your thought groups?

Rules and Practices 2: Blending and Linking

In rapid speech, when one word is blended with the next, two or
three sounds cluster together. Some sounds are lost, some are added,
some shift to different words, and some are spoken almost simul-
tanously.

Most sound changes are far too complex to learn consciously, but
they may occur automatically if you make an effort to blend or link
words in the same thought group together.

A few of the more useful rules for blending and linking follow.
These guidelines will help your comprehension as well as your pronunciation of English.

Rule 10-4

☑ When consecutive words in the same thought group end and begin
with the same consonant sound, the sound is held or lengthened, not
pronounced twice.

Examples: at‿twelve   (hold *t*)

   big‿game   (hold *g*)

   keep‿peace   (hold *p*)

   this‿song   (lengthen *s*)

   he'll‿look   (lengthen *l*)

   with‿three   (lengthen *th*)

*From *The First Lunar Landing as Told by the Astronauts, 20th Anniversary,* National
Aeronautics and Space Administration, Office of Public Affairs, 1989, p. 21.

Rule 10-5

☑ When a word begins with a vowel sound, borrow the final consonant sound from the previous word in the same thought group.

Examples: pick͜ it͜ up   = pi   ki   tup

check͜ it͜ off = che   ki   toff

drop ͜h͟im͜ off = dro   pi   moff

Rule 10-6

☑ The stop consonants, /p/ and /b/, /k/ and /g/, and /t/ and /d/, at the ends of words are spoken at almost the same time as the first consonant sounds in the next words.

Examples: cab͜ driver   (hold /b/ until you are ready to say /d/)

lab͜ technician

stop͜ sign

keep͜ trying

lap͜ top͜ computer

look͜ like

big͜ problem

EXERCISE 4

To practice linking and blending, repeat these phrases after the speaker on the tape or your teacher, or practice with a partner.

Examples: cub͜ scouts   (hold /b/ until you are ready to say /s/)

help͜ out   (move the /p/ to the next word)

keep͜ promises   (hold the /p/)

job͜ training	look͜ tired
job͜ ladder	look͜ sick
job͜ offer	look͜ up
job͜ benefits	look͜ carefully

lab_coat	big_debt
lab_assistant	big_meeting
lab_equipment	big_game
lab_procedures	big_organization
help_teach	got_caught
help_make	got_thirsty
help_organize	got_tired
help_people	got_arrested
deep_trouble	caused_misunderstanding
deep_water	caused_problems
deep_thinker	caused_deaths
deep_in debt	caused_anxiety

Rule 10-7

Listen to these questions. What sound change do you hear when *t* is blended with *y*?

Examples: Don't_you know?

Haven't_you heard?

Can't_you go?

☑ When a word ends in /t/ and the next word begins with /y/, the blended sound is /tʃ/ as in *ch*oose. This sound combination is common in negative questions.

Rule 10-8

What sound change occurs when *d* is blended with *y* in these short sentences?

Examples: Did_you know?

Would_you come?

Could_you help?

I called_you.

☑ When a word ends in /d/ and the next word begins with /y/, the blended sound is /dʒ/ as in *j*uice. This sound combination is common in past tense questions and questions with *could, should,* and *would.*

Communicative Practice 1: Driving Test

Use thought groups and blending as you give your partner an oral driving test.

One partner should mark questions one through six for thought groups (/) and blending (‿). The other partner should mark questions seven through twelve. Practice the questions until the thought groups sound natural and the blending is smooth. Ask your partner the questions you marked. Write your partner's answers.

Preview blending in these thought groups:

. . . should‿you walk‿on   . . . set‿your headlights

. . . if you start‿to skid   . . . should‿you exchange

. . . should‿you use   . . . what should‿you do

. . . how should‿you

DRIVING TEST

1. If there are no sidewalks, which side of the street should you walk on?

2. Unless otherwise posted, what is the maximum speed limit in your state?

3. If you start to skid on a slippery surface, should you use your brakes?

4. How should you set your headlights in fog?

5. If you are involved in an accident with another driver, what information should you exchange?

6. If you have been drinking alcohol, what should you do before you drive?

7. If you get drowsy while driving, what should you do?

8. If you see a flashing red light at an intersection, what should you do?

9. If you see a flashing yellow light at an intersection, what should you do?

10. If your brakes fail, what should you do?

11. What is the minimum speed on the freeway in your state?

12. If there is trouble ahead, how should you warn the driver behind you?

Compare your answers to your classmates'. Some driving laws vary from state to state. You may need to consult the driver's manual for your state if you are unsure of an answer.

Communicative Practice 2: News Broadcast

Find a news story of interest in the newspaper or in a news magazine. Write a summary of the story below. Divide the sentences into logical thought groups with slash marks (/).

Make a list of key words below that might be difficult for you to pronounce. Look up the words in your dictionary and practice saying them silently in their respective thought groups. Rehearse the story until it sounds natural.

Imagine that you are a news broadcaster. Tape yourself reading your news story. Listen to your tape. Did you deliver the information in meaningful thought groups?

NEWS BROADCAST

_____

_____

_____

_____

_____

_____

_____

_____

_____

_____

_____

_____

_____

_____

LIST OF DIFFICULT WORDS

_____   _____

_____   _____

_____   _____

Locate the focus of each thought group (the last stressed word or syllable of each thought group). Locate the focus of each sentence (the last stressed word or syllable of each sentence). Read the broadcast again. Did your slight pitch fall occur on each thought group focus? Did your deep pitch fall occur on each sentence focus?

When native speakers read or give a rehearsed presentation, thought groups sound smooth and close to the ideal. In spontaneous speech, however, speakers of American English frequently hesitate while planning what they are going to say or while searching for a word that they need. These hesitations often interfere with thought groups.

Hesitations and repetitions, if not excessive, are a normal, expected part of spontaneous speech. Most native speakers never eliminate hesitations in their speech, and you probably won't either.

Extend Your Skills . . . to a Process Presentation

Explain a process from sports, your daily life, or your field of work or study. Choose a process that is interesting to you and your class, that has at least three distinct steps, and that can be explained clearly in about three to five minutes (i.e., the correct way to eat Japanese noodles, how to take a good close-up photograph, how to hit a backhand in tennis, how to move blocks of text on a word processor, how to use a FAX machine, how to make a perfect bowl of popcorn).

The presentation will provide an opportunity to use **all** the skills learned in this course; however, the primary purpose of the explanation is to practice the following:

1. The use of transition words like *first, next, after that,* and *finally* to signal each new step of the process.

2. The use of transition words like *that is, in other words, to repeat,* and *to say it another way* to signal repetition and rephrasing of important information in your presentation.

3. The use of pitch fall and pause to mark thought groups, especially to set off transition words and repeated or rephrased information.

4. Brief pauses to set off major segments of your presentation (i.e., between each step in your process).

Outline your presentation on a notecard. For each step in your process, you might want to tell the audience **what** the step is, **why** it is important, and **how** you accomplish it. Use visual aids (simple outlines, diagrams, pictures, or flow charts) to add interest and clarity.

Rehearse your presentation several times using only your outline. Use a simple, clear, direct speaking style.

Videotape or audiotape your presentation. Be sure to look at your audience during your presentation. Evaluate the recording using the form that follows. Submit the form to your teacher.

Process Presentation/Self-Evaluation Form

Name: _____

Topic: _____

Scoring Form: Listen to your tape. Assign one point for each component below. You may need to listen to your tape several times.

A. Delivery   **1 point each**

1. Attention to time limit   _____

2. Well-organized   _____

   —Clear introduction

   —Effective transitions

   —Clear conclusion

3. Repetition/rephrasing   _____

4. Interesting   _____

5. Appropriate level of complexity   _____

TOTAL (Part A)   _____ × 10 = _____

B. Pronunciation/Clarity   **1 point each**

1. Clear consonants and vowels in key words _____

2. Good stress in key words   _____

3. Effective sentence stress and focus   _____

4. Appropriate thought groups/pausing   _____

5. Adequate speed and volume   _____

TOTAL (Part B)   _____ × 10 = _____

TOTAL (Part A + Part B)   _____%

Comments:

Oral Review: Phrasing, Pausing, and Blending

Name_____

Schedule an individual consultation with your teacher, complete the review as a group project, or submit the review on tape.

Part A

Finish these five clauses, using good phrasing and linking. This sentence completion activity is good practice for the Test of Spoken English (TSE).

1. After they finished dinner,

2. Because he failed his test,

3. If you're going to leave,

4. Since it was broken,

5. If I were a _____,

Part B

You have been asked to order the following items for your department at work.

Carousel Slide Projector and Viewer. Projects onto internal screen or regular projection screen. Uses 80 or 140 capacity slide tray (not included).
#4120TLC $299.97

Computer Work Center with Hutch. Large work surface with adjustable monitor shelf. Full modesty panel.
#78211V $187.00

Your department needs immediate delivery so you have to order by phone and leave the order on an answering machine. Call the office supply company and leave the following information. Organize your information into thought groups, paying particular attention to grouping long numbers.

1. Your name

2. Your company

3. Item 1: Item name, quantity, catalogue number, cost

4. Item 2: Item name, quantity, catalogue number, cost

5. Mailing address: number and street

                                     city, state, and zipcode

6. Your phone number (_ _ _ ' _ _ _ _ _ _ _)

   Your fax number   (_ _ _ _ _ _ _ _ _ _)

7. Type of credit card

   Name on card

   Card number * (_ _ _ _ _ _ _ _ _ _ _ _ _ _ _ _)

   Expiration date (_ _ _ _)

                    month/year

*Make up a 16-digit number.

Listen to your tape before you submit it. Did you use thought groups? Did you blend words within thought groups? Make corrections at the end of the tape.

Beyond the Pronunciation Class

In this course, most of you have become aware of how to speak more clearly. Some of you have begun to make changes in your pronunciation, both conscious and unconscious, when speaking in class. Others have begun to make changes in pronunciation outside of class.

Unlearning old ways of speaking and learning new ways of speaking require continued practice in many different contexts. Here are some suggestions to help you retain the progress you have made and to continue to make long-term progress on your own.

Suggestion 1

Reestablish your commitment to **take the time** and **make the conscious effort** to change. It won't happen automatically.

WHAT YOU CAN DO

1. Look at the *Pronunciation Proficiency Continuum* in Chapter 1. Where were you at the beginning of the course? Where are you now? Where do you want to be in six months?

2. Look at the practice priorities in your *Speech Profile Summary Form* in Chapter 1 and your *Mid-Course Self-Evaluation* at the end of Chapter 6. What are your current practice priorities? Write them below. Review your practice priorities every two or three weeks.

   a. _____

   b. _____

   c. _____

Many of the principles and practice strategies included in Appendix A are based on the ideas and insights of Joan Morley and William Acton. See the *Teacher's Manual* for a list of references.

Suggestion 2

Try to overcome any resistance you have to sounding like a speaker of American English. Such resistance might be an obstacle to pronunciation progress.

Changing pronunciation patterns involves changes in breathing, facial expression, and sometimes even body movement. You may feel less Korean, Chinese, Japanese, French, Indian, Thai, German, Greek, Italian, Arabic, Latin American, or Spanish when you speak English, but be assured that you won't lose your accent completely. You will probably always sound like a speaker of your native language.

WHAT YOU CAN DO

1. Imitate American English speakers you know and admire. Try to mimic gestures and facial expressions as well as specific pronunciation patterns.

2. Imagine your use of American English speech patterns to be like a coat that you can put on and take off at will or as the situation requires.

3. Remember that your goals are to change only those patterns that interfere with understanding and that are highly distracting to the listener.

Suggestion 3

Practice regularly in order to achieve long-term changes in your pronunciation.

WHAT YOU CAN DO

1. Schedule a five- to ten-minute practice session each day. Focus on your practice priorities.

   • Practice a new sound or stress pattern in words and phrases silently or in slow motion. Focus on how the pattern feels.

   • Practice a new sound or stress pattern out loud but with your eyes closed. Focus on how the pattern sounds.

   • Practice a new sound or stress pattern in sentences. Read the sentence, and then look up and say it.

   • Practice a sound or rhythm pattern in an oral reading. Mark the reading for thought groups and for occurrences of a particular sound, stress, or rhythm pattern. Record the reading, listen to it, and evaluate it.

   • Anticipate and rehearse what you will say in a class, in a meeting, in a discussion, in a phone conversation, or in an oral presentation.

Record it and listen to it. Monitor your pronunciation of key words related to the topic.

- Practice in front of a mirror. Try to mimic the mouth and facial movement of speakers of American English.

- Record yourself reading a passage of at least 300 words from your field of work or study. Listen to the recording and take notes as if in a lecture. Write the important content words and omit the less important function words. Listen again and evaluate your use of overall rhythm patterns. Did you stress the content words and reduce the function words?

2. Self-monitor your speech for a short time each day. Since it takes concentrated effort to be conscious of what you are saying **and** how you are saying it, don't try to self-monitor much longer than five minutes each day. Choose a relaxed situation in which you have some control over the conversation.

3. Do not be anxious about errors. If you hear one, note it and go on. If it is convenient to self-correct, do so.

4. Use a technique called tracking. In tracking, try to repeat what a speaker of American English is saying on a word-for-word basis, following about one or two words behind the speaker. At first, follow the intonation contours, speed, stress, and rhythm patterns by humming. As you become better at tracking, add words. You can track speakers on radio and television as well as in real situations. You can track silently or out loud. If the situation allows, it is also useful to mirror the body movements and facial expressions of the speaker.

5. Seek the support of speakers of American English. Tell trusted friends and co-workers that you have taken a course to improve your pronunciation. Tell them how they can assist you. Tell them that you want to know when they don't understand you. Tell them if you want to be corrected.

6. Help speakers of American English to be good informants and models. If you ask English speakers how to pronounce words, their models may be exaggerated and unnatural. Ask the informants to say words in sentences and you will probably hear more natural pronunciations.

7. Keep an oral diary or journal. Record thoughts and events of the day on a cassette. Evaluate the recording by focusing on one pronunciation feature at a time. Listen for clear, as well as unclear, productions of particular pronunciation points.

8. Keep a list of words that you encounter frequently and that you want to say clearly. Consult your dictionary for pronunciations. Practice the words often by saying them aloud once, then twice in a row, then three times in a row, and so on. Create typical sentences for the words, or ask an English speaker to record the words in sentences for you so that you can practice by imitating the model or speaking along with the model.

Consonants

An Overview of the Consonant Sounds of American English

The Twenty-Four Consonant Sounds

The consonant sounds of American English are represented below with the phonetic symbols used in the *Longman Dictionary of American English** and with key words.

Repeat the sounds and the key words after your teacher or the speaker on tape.

/p/ **p**ie	/f/ **f**an	/ʃ/ **sh**oe	/ŋ/ ri**ng**
/b/ **b**uy	/v/ **v**an	/ʒ/ u**s**ual	/l/ **l**ed
/t/ **t**ime	/θ/ **th**ink	/tʃ/ **ch**oose	/r/ **r**ed
/d/ **d**ime	/ð/ **th**em	/dʒ/ **j**uice	/w/ **w**e
/k/ **k**ey	/s/ **s**o	/m/ **m**y	/y/ **y**ou
/g/ **g**o	/z/ **z**oo	/n/ **n**o	/h/ **h**ow

1. Circle the consonant sounds that you do **not** have in your native language.

2. Refer to your *Speech Profile Summary Form* in Chapter 1. List the consonant sounds your teacher indicated were troublesome for you.

   _____   _____   _____

3. List any other consonant sounds that are difficult for you.

   _____   _____   _____

Longman Dictionary of American English, White Plains, NY: Longman, 1983.

Voiced and Voiceless Consonants

One of the ways consonants are classified is by whether they are voiced or voiceless. When you say a voiced consonant, the vocal cords vibrate. When you say a voiceless consonant, the vocal cords don't vibrate.

The meanings of many words depend on whether a consonant is voiced or not. The primary difference between the eight pairs of consonants below is whether they are voiceless or voiced.

Repeat the word pairs below. Monitor for voicing by placing your fingers on your throat or your cheeks to feel the vibration of the vocal cords.

VOICELESS CONSONANTS		VOICED CONSONANTS	
/p/	**p**ath	/b/	**b**ath
/t/	**t**ime	/d/	**d**ime
/k/	**c**ame	/g/	**g**ame
/f/	**f**an	/v/	**v**an
/θ/	**th**ink	/ð/	**th**em
/s/	pri**c**e	/z/	pri**z**e
/ʃ/	**sh**oe	/ʒ/	u**s**ual
/tʃ/	**ch**in	/dʒ/	**g**in

Except for the voiceless /h/, the remaining consonants are voiced and have no voiceless counterparts: /m/, /n/, /ŋ/, /l/, /r/, and /y/, and /w/.

✔ The most important difference between voiceless and voiced consonants at the **ends** of words is that **the vowel sounds longer before a voiced consonant.**

1. Listen to your teacher or the speaker on tape say the word pairs below and circle the word in each pair that seems to have a longer vowel sound.

ri**p**	ri**b**
we**d**	we**t**
ri**ch**	ri**dg**e
ba**dg**e	ba**tch**
fa**c**e	pha**s**e
led	**le**t
plu**g**	plu**ck**
lea**f**	lea**v**e
hal**f**	ha**v**e
righ**t**	ri**d**e
sa**v**e	sa**f**e
play**s**	pla**c**e

Check the *Answer Key.*

Repeat the word pairs above.

At the **beginning** and in the **middle** of words, the most important difference between voiceless and voiced consonants is that **voiceless consonants are usually pronounced with the sound of escaping air or aspiration.**

2. Listen to your teacher or the speaker on tape say the pairs of words below. Circle the word in each pair with the consonant that has **more** of a sound of escaping air.

*v*iew	*f*ew
ser*v*ice	sur*f*ace
*f*an	*v*an
*b*ore	*p*oor
a*pp*ear	a *b*eer
*p*ack	*b*ack
*g*lass	*c*lass
*c*ome	*g*um
*d*rip	*t*rip
*t*ime	*d*ime
*ch*eap	*j*eep
*ch*oke	*j*oke

Check the *Answer Key*.

Repeat the phrasal pairs below after your teacher or the speaker on tape. Pay special attention to aspiration in the voiceless sounds.

VOICELESS (ASPIRATED)	VOICED (UNASPIRATED)
f	**v**
the last *f*ew	the last *v*iew
fix the *f*an	fix the *v*an
re*f*use the offer	re*v*iews the offer
dangerous ri*f*le	dangerous ri*v*al
p	**b**
*p*ack it up	*b*ack it up
select a *p*each	select a *b*each
*p*ouring rain	*b*oring rain
a good *p*ie	a good *b*uy
k	**g**
*c*ould swim	*g*ood swim
a full *c*lass	a full *g*lass
useless *c*lue	useless *g*lue
ba*ck*ing the purchase	ba*gg*ing the purchase

Forming Consonant Sounds

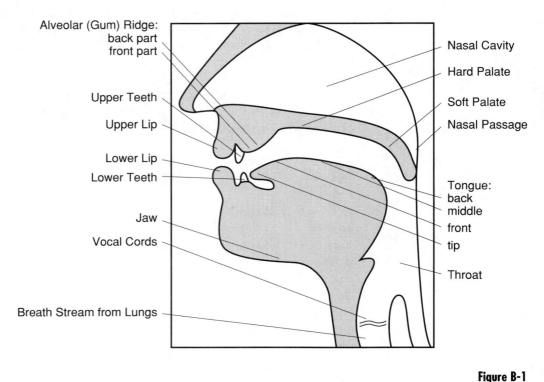

Figure B-1

These organs of speech are used to pronounce consonants.

Consonants are formed by partially or completely blocking the breath stream with the lips, tongue, gum ridge, palate (roof of the mouth), or throat. Some consonants involve completely stopping the breath stream, then abruptly releasing it. These sounds are short and are sometimes called stops. Say these stops: /p/, /b/, /t/, /d/, /k/, and /g/. Some consonants involve a *partial* obstruction or constriction of the breath stream. When the breath stream is constricted, consonants are longer in duration and are sometimes called continuants. Say these continuants: /θ/, /ð/, /s/, /z/, /ʃ/, /ʒ/, /f/, and /v/.

Listen to the word pairs. Notice the shorter duration of the stops and the longer duration of the continuants.

STOPS (SHORTER SOUNDS)	CONTINUANTS (LONGER SOUNDS)
lea**p**	lea**f**
wi**t**	wi**th**
fi**g**	fi**sh**
ba**k**e	bei**g**e
bea**d**	bee**f**
dea**d**	dea**th**

Two consonant sounds, /tʃ/ and /dʒ/, are a combination of a stop plus a continuant. The /tʃ/ is a /t/ + /ʃ/. Say /ʃ/ . . . /ʃ/ . . . /ʃ/. Now put your tongue in position for /t/ before you release the /ʃ/ and say /tʃ/ . . . /tʃ/ . . . /tʃ/.

The /dʒ/ is a /d/ + /ʒ/. Say /ʒ/ . . . /ʒ/ . . . /ʒ/. Now put your tongue in position for /d/ before you release the /ʒ/ and say /dʒ/ . . . /dʒ/ . . . /dʒ/.

Some continuants involve directing the breath stream through the nose. Say /m/, /n/, and /ŋ/ and feel the breath stream escape through your nose. One continuant, /l/, involves directing the breath stream around the sides of the tongue. Some continuants, namely /r/, /w/, and /y/, involve the organs of speech gliding from one position to another depending on the surrounding sounds.

The chart below summarizes the formation of consonant sounds. Speaking, however, is a complicated, dynamic process and mouth movements can vary for each sound depending on the speaker, the surrounding sounds, and the formality of the situation.

	Both Lips	Lip-Teeth	Tongue-Teeth	Tongue-Gum Ridge	Tongue-Hard Palate	Tongue-Soft Palate	Throat
Breath is Stopped and Released	p/b			t/d		k/g	
Breath is Constricted		f/v	θ/ð	s/z	ʃ/ʒ		h
Breath is Stopped and Constricted					tʃ/dʒ		
Breath is Released through Nose	m			n		ŋ	
Breath is Released over Sides of Tongue				l			
Mouth Glides from one Position to Another	w				y r		

Consonant Practices

This section provides concentrated practice with consonant sounds that are especially troublesome for advanced speakers and most likely to cause misunderstanding if pronounced incorrectly.

Five consonant sounds are reviewed and contrasted with sounds that many learners of English use as replacements.

Consonant 1: /θ/ as in *think* (vs. /s/, /t/, and /f/)
Consonant 2: /f/ as in *fine* (vs. /p/)
Consonant 3: /ʃ/ as in *she* (vs. /tʃ/ and /s/)
Consonant 4: /r/ as in *right* (vs. /l/)
Consonant 5: /v/ as in *vote* (vs. /w/, /b/, and /f/)

Each consonant review includes a *Listen* section and an *Exercise* section for independent laboratory use, as well as a *Communicative Practice* section for follow-up classroom practice in pairs or small groups. If you are having difficulty with consonant sounds not included below, ask your teacher to recommend practice material from a textbook that presents a survey of all speech sounds.

Consonant One: /θ/ as in *think* (vs. /s/, /t/, and /f/)

1. Learners of English sometimes replace the voiceless /θ/ with an /s/, /t/, or /f/ so that *thank* sounds like *sank, thought* sounds like *taught,* or *three* sounds like *free.* Other learners of English sometimes omit the sound entirely at the ends of words.

2. The voiceless /θ/ occurs in content words. In contrast, the voiced /ð/ occurs primarily in function words (e.g., the, this, that) and a few family relation words (e.g., mother, brother).

LISTENING ACTIVITY 1

Listen to the /θ/. Notice the friction-like sound of the breath stream as it passes over the tongue between the teeth.

/θ/ . . . /θ/ . . . /θ/ . . . /θ/ . . . /θ/

LISTENING ACTIVITY 2

Listen to the words with /θ/. Do you hear the sound at the beginning (B), in the middle (M), or at the end (E) of each word? Close your books and write B, M or E on a piece of paper. Check the *Answer Key.*

a. think	e. death	i. south
b. three	f. anything	j. length
c. bath	g. Thursday	k. birthday
d. mathematics	h. thirty	l. month

LISTENING ACTIVITY 3

Listen to the word pairs. Which word of each pair has the /θ/ sound —
the first or the second? Close your books and write 1 or 2 on a piece of
paper. Check the *Answer Key.*

a. think   sink   f. path   pass
b. math   mass   g. sought   thought
c. truce   truth   h. youth   you
d. three   tree   i. tense   tenth
e. mat   math   j. thin   fin

LISTENING ACTIVITY 4

Listen to the sentences with one of the words in parentheses. Mark the
correct response/meaning. Check the *Answer Key.*

a. I think it's (thin/tin).

_____ It's not thick.

_____ It's not aluminum.

b. She took a (bat/bath).

_____ She wants to play baseball.

_____ She was dirty.

c. It's a (three/tree).

_____ It's not an 8.

_____ It's not a bush.

d. I think she'll be (three/free).

_____ I'm almost certain she's two now.

_____ Her calendar looks clear.

e. Help him. He's (sinking/thinking).

_____ He can't swim.

_____ He can't solve the problem alone.

LISTENING ACTIVITY 5

Listen to the paragraph. Fill in the blanks with words that have /θ/.
Check the *Answer Key*.

What Makes You Thin?

What makes you _____? Most people
_____ that dieting is the answer, but researchers say
that exercise is the best way to be _____. In one study
_____ men who were sedentary were put on an exercise
program. They walked, jogged, and ran _____ the
one-year program. The first _____ the study showed
was that the men who had exercised the most lost the most weight.
The second _____ the study revealed was that the
men who lost the most weight ate more too. The researchers
_____ that fat people don't really eat a lot. Their problem is that they are inactive.

Figure B-2
Forming the voiceless /θ/. Place
the tip of the tongue against the
cutting edge of the upper teeth.
Then force air through the contact.

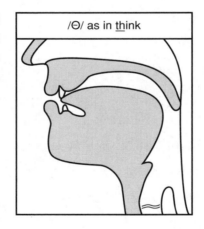

/Θ/ as in think

EXERCISE 1

Repeat the words with /θ/.

think	something	with
thought	without	both
three	anything	strength
thirsty	birthday	truth
through	worthwhile	south
thank	hypothesis	north
Thursday	method	math
theory	withhold	width

EXERCISE 2

a. Words that contain both /θ/ and /s/, /t/, or /f/ may be especially difficult. Repeat these words.

With /s/	*With /t/*	*With /f/*
south	teeth	fourth
something	truth	fifth
synthesize	twentieth	thief
thesis	thirty	faith

b. Consonant clusters with /θ/ might also be difficult. The θ is a continuant so you need to continue the θ (or keep the breath stream flowing) right into the next consonant in the sequence. Repeat these words.

three	bir**ths**
throw	mon**ths**
through	nor**thw**est

EXERCISE 3 Choose three words with /θ/ that you use frequently. Write a typical phrase or sentence you might say with each of the words. Practice each sentence three times.

a. _____

b. _____

c. _____

EXERCISE 4

Repeat the word pairs in Listening Activity 3. Make a clear distinction between /θ/ and /s/, /f/, and /t/.

EXERCISE 5

Practice blending the final /θ/ in words with the first sound of the next word. Repeat the phrases. Say each phrase as if it were one word.

fourth‿thing	with‿three colleagues
fourth‿sentence	with‿them
fourth‿point	with‿my friends
fourth‿house	with‿time
fourth‿time	with‿confidence
fourth‿order	with‿a knife

EXERCISE 6

Practice the italicized words silently. Repeat the sentences. Look up from your book as you say each sentence.

a. I'm so ***thirsty.***

b. That was ***three*** days ago.

c. The test is on ***Thursday.***

d. He grew up in the ***southwest.***

e. Give me one ***method*** for solving the problem.

f. It's not ***worth*** your time.

g. We talked about two ***things.***

h. I'm sorry. I have ***something*** else to do right now.

EXERCISE 7

Record yourself reading the paragraph titled "What Makes You Thin?" in Listening Activity 5 in the *Answer Key.* Monitor the italicized words with /θ/.

COMMUNICATIVE PRACTICE 1

Imagine that you are a teaching assistant in an American university. You have to announce a schedule change for a design methods course. Use the information in the memo below.

Mark and practice all words and numbers with the voiceless /θ/ before you begin. Work with a partner and take turns making the announcement. Converting a written schedule into a spoken announcement is good practice for the Test of Spoken English (TSE).

MEMORANDUM

TO: All Design Methods 634 Teaching Assistants
RE: Schedule Change

Please make your students aware of the following changes effective September 19:

	Former Time	*New Time*
Discussion Section A	Thurs., 8:30 p.m. Classroom Bldg. Room 18	Thurs., 4:30 p.m. Classroom Bldg. Room 23
Discussion Section B	Tues., 2:00 p.m. French Bldg. Room 222	Tues., 2:30 p.m. Thurmond Hall Room 353

COMMUNICATIVE PRACTICE 2   In a small group, discuss which occupations below have the best outlook for job growth and future employment. Each member of the group should rank the following ten jobs, from the one with the most promising future (first) to the least promising future (tenth). Report to your group how you ranked each occupation and justify your rankings.

Preview and self-monitor your pronunciation of ordinal numbers (third, fourth, fifth, etc.), phrases used in expressing a point of view (I think . . . , I don't think . . . ,), key terms (growth), and occupational names (author, mathematician, etc.).

Check the *Answer Key* to find out how the jobs were ranked according to *The Jobs Rated Almanac.*

OCCUPATIONS

Computer Programmer	Construction Worker
Bank Teller	Auto Painter
Dairy Farmer	College Professor
Mathematician	Surgeon
Airplane Pilot	Book Author

RANK: OCCUPATION

Most Promising Growth

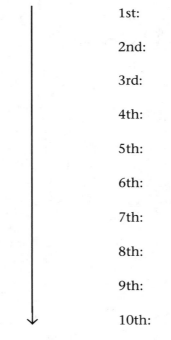

1st:

2nd:

3rd:

4th:

5th:

6th:

7th:

8th:

9th:

10th:

Least Promising Growth

Consonant Two: /f/ as in *fine* (vs. /p/)

1. The /f/ sound is spelled *f* (free), *ph* (sphere), and *gh* (tough).

2. Students sometimes replace the /f/ with /p/ so that *coffee* sounds like *copy*.

LISTENING ACTIVITY 1

Listen to /f/. Notice the friction-like sound as the breath is forced between the upper teeth and lower lip.

/f/ . . . /f/ . . . /f/ . . . /f/ . . . /f/

LISTENING ACTIVITY 2

Listen to the words with /f/. Is the /f/ at the beginning (B), in the middle (M), or at the end (E) of each word? Close your books and write B, M, or E on a piece of paper. Check the *Answer Key.*

a. find	e. proof	i. fine
b. half	f. reflect	j. belief
c. first	g. specific	k. few
d. golf	h. fix	l. yourself

LISTENING ACTIVITY 3

Listen to the word pairs. Does the first or second word of each pair have the /f/ sound? Close your books and write 1 or 2 on a piece of paper. Check the *Answer Key.*

a. fine	pine	g. pan	fan
b. coffee	copy	h. cheap	chief
c. paint	faint	i. fill	pill
d. past	fast	j. pool	fool
e. peel	feel	k. leafing	leaping
f. fashion	passion	l. fact	pact

LISTENING ACTIVITY 4

Listen to the sentences with one of the words in parentheses. Mark the correct response/meaning. Check the *Answer Key.*

a. It's a new (copy, coffee) machine.

_____ That's why the copies are so clear.

_____ That's why the coffee tastes so good.

b. It's a (fact, pact).

_____ Do you have proof?

_____ Is everyone in agreement?

c. That's the (chief, cheap) executive officer.

_____ That's the big boss.

_____ We never get raises.

d. She's driving (past, fast).

_____ Did you see her go by?

_____ She should slow down.

e. Excuse me. Where would I find (pans, fans)?

_____ In the housewares department.

_____ In the small appliances department.

LISTENING ACTIVITY 5

Listen to the paragraph. Fill in the blanks with words that have the /f/ sound. Check the *Answer Key.*

VideoPhones

In 1992, AT&T began _____ customers a Video-

_____, a _____ with a small color screen

that allows callers to look at each other while they are talking.

_____ callers, however, _____ to be in-

visible, there is a special _____ that will close the lens of

the camera. Now, in addition to the popular _____ for

your cars and video _____ _____ systems

that have become almost standard in the _____ of big

businesses, you can plug Video _____ into standard

_____ outlets in your home.

Figure B-3
Forming the voiceless /f/. Lightly touch the upper front teeth to the inside lower lip. Force air through the light contact.

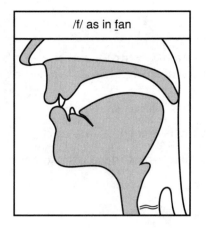

/f/ as in <u>f</u>an

EXERCISE 1

Repeat these words with /f/.

few	confuse	proof
function	effective	staff
first	reference	golf
feedback	different	half
fix	therefore	if
free	careful	graph
fail	office	relief
frequently	transfer	beef

EXERCISE 2

a. Words that contain both /f/ and /p/ might be difficult. Repeat these words:

friendship, follow-up, profession, payoff, playoff, proof, prefer, perfect

b. Consonant clusters with /f/ might also be difficult. Repeat these words.

flew	le**ft**
free	so**ft**
from	stu**ff**ed
flaw	gra**ph**s

EXERCISE 3 Choose three words with /f/ that you use frequently. Write a typical sentence you might say with each of the words. Practice saying each sentence three times.

a. _____

b. _____

c. _____

EXERCISE 4

  Say the word pairs in Listening Activity 3. Make a clear distinction between /f/ and /p/.

EXERCISE 5

  Practice blending the final /f/ with the first sound of the next word in the phrases below. Repeat the phrases. Say each phrase as if it were one word.

half_finished	staff_facilities
half_cooked	staff_supplies
half_done	staff_complaints
half_typed	staff_meeting
half_a cup	staff_involvement

EXERCISE 6

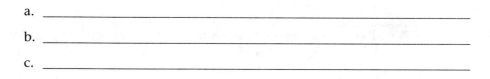 Practice the italicized words silently. Repeat the sentences. Look up from the book as you say the sentences.

a. I'm ***fine.***

b. Which do you ***prefer***?

c. What's the ***first*** term?

d. Did you ***fill*** out the ***form***?

e. There are a ***few*** exceptions.

f. Were you ***satisfied*** with his explanation?

g. Have you ***found*** a place to live?

h. We need a new ***coffee*** machine for the ***office.***

EXERCISE 3   Record yourself reading the paragraph titled "VideoPhones" in Listening Activity 5 in the *Answer Key.* Monitor your pronunciation of the *underlined* words with /f/.

COMMUNICATIVE PRACTICE   Predict consequences by completing the unfinished "if" statements. In groups of five or six, share completed sentences. Which responses were the most common, the most unusual, the most humorous, and the most interesting?

Monitor your pronunciation of *if* and other words with /f/: freeways, professors, four, twenty-four, fly, for, and found. Sentence completion activities are good practice for the Test of Spoken English (TSE).

1. If the speed limits on freeways are increased to 70 miles per hour, . . .

2. If a cure for AIDS is found, . . .

3. If electric cars become popular, . . .

4. If most of the talented professors work for private business, . . .

5. If I could fly anywhere in the world, . . .

6. If the unemployment rate rises, . . .

7. If I had only 24 hours to live, . . .

8. If the work week is shortened to four days, . . .

9. If I could buy the car of my choice, . . .

10. If _____

Consonant Three: /ʃ/ as in *she* (vs. /tʃ/ and /s/)

1. The /ʃ/ has many spellings. The most common is *sh* (she), but /ʃ/ can also be spelled *-ti-* (nation), *-ci-* (social), *-ssi-* (mission), and *-ssu-* (issue).

2. Some students replace /ʃ/ with /tʃ/ so that *share* sounds like *chair*. Other students replace /ʃ/ with /s/ so that *shine* sounds like *sign*.

LISTENING ACTIVITY 1

Listen to the /ʃ/ sound. Notice the easy, slow release of breath.

/ʃ/ . . . /ʃ/ . . . /ʃ/ . . . /ʃ/ . . .

LISTENING ACTIVITY 2

Listen to the words with /ʃ/. Do you hear the /ʃ/ at the beginning (B), in the middle (M), or at the end (E) of each word? Close your books and write B, M, or E on a piece of paper. Check the *Answer Key*.

a. share	f. cash
b. sure	g. special
c. rush	h. Spanish
d. push	i. washing
e. official	j. permission

LISTENING ACTIVITY 3

Listen to the word pairs. Is the /ʃ/ sound in the first or the second word? Close your books and write 1 or 2 on a piece of paper. Check the *Answer Key*.

a. sheet	seat	f. shift	sift
b. shoe	chew	g. shore	chore
c. see	she	h. watching	washing
d. sheet	cheat	i. sour	shower
e. chop	shop	j. catch	cash

LISTENING ACTIVITY 4

Listen to the sentences with one of the words in parentheses. Mark the correct response/meaning. Check the *Answer Key.*

a. What's he (washing, watching)?

_____His sheets.

_____A football game.

b. It's going to (shower, sour).

_____Is rain predicted?

_____Should I put it in the refrigerator?

c. Can you (catch, cash) this?

_____Sure. I used to play baseball.

_____Sure. I'm going to the bank.

d. She feels the (shame, same).

_____Even though it wasn't her fault.

_____She's in complete agreement.

LISTENING ACTIVITY 5

Listen to the following paragraph. Fill in the blanks with words that have the /ʃ/ sound. Check the *Answer Key.*

Shyness

About 92 million Americans are _____. Researchers are taking an interest in _____ and have
reached a number of different conclusions. According to one study,
_____ _____ these days are more
complex and _____ is becoming a _____
concern. Another study found that only about half of the
_____ people were tense or _____ in
_____ _____, contrary to popular belief.
And still another found that _____ people tend to be
more stable in their _____. Some psychologists think
that _____ may be inherited, while others think that
_____ is cultural.

Figure B-4
Forming the voiceless /ʃ/ sound. Start by saying /s/. Then pull the tip of the tongue back slightly and created a broad groove with the tongue. Protrude and round the lips slightly. Direct the breathstream over the middle of the tongue.

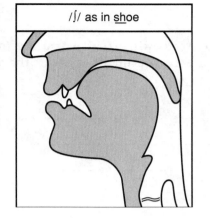

/ʃ/ as in <u>sh</u>oe

EXERCISE 1

Repeat these words.

she	refreshing	foolish
short	machine	crash
shelf	washing	finish
shower	official	fresh
should	social	push
shoe	patient	British
shop	vacation	fish
shampoo	national	selfish

EXERCISE 2

Words that contain both /ʃ/ and /s/ or /tʃ/ are difficult for some students. Repeat these words.

situation, selfish, social, section, special, insurance

Verbs ending in /ʃ/ followed by the -*ing* are also sometimes difficult. Repeat these verbs until they sound natural.

cashing, wishing, pushing, punishing, washing, fishing, finishing, refreshing, rushing

EXERCISE 3

Choose three words with /ʃ/ that you use frequently. Write a typical phrase or sentence you might say with the words. Practice each sentence three times.

a. _____

b. _____

c. _____

EXERCISE 4

Repeat the word pairs in Listening Activity 3. Make a clear distinction between /ʃ/ and /s/ and between /ʃ/ and /tʃ/.

EXERCISE 5

Practice blending the final /ʃ/ in words with the first sound of the next word. Repeat the phrases. Say each phrase as if it were one word.

wash‿sheets	finish‿shopping
wash‿dishes	finish‿studying
wash‿your hands	finish‿talking
wash‿the clothes	finish‿eating
wash‿up	finish‿exercising

EXERCISE 6

Practice the italicized words silently. Repeat the sentences. Look up from your book as you say each sentence.

a. Please pass the ***sugar.***

b. The tickets ***should*** come in the mail.

c. I'll have to ***rush*** to ***finish*** before the deadline.

d. We had time between ***shifts*** for a ***short*** lunch.

e. ***She's*** fluent in ***English*** and ***Spanish.***

f. She's ***anxious*** to ***show*** you her new office.

g. Is the *fish* ***fresh***?

h. ***She's*** applied for a ***fellowship.***

EXERCISE 7   Record yourself reading the paragraph titled "Shyness" in Listening Activity 5 in the *Answer Key*. Monitor your pronunciation of the italicized words with /ʃ/.

COMMUNICATIVE PRACTICE   In small groups of three to five students, compare and contrast the university systems in each of your countries. Monitor your pronunciation of /ʃ/ in key terms during your discussion. Share highlights of your group's discussion with the class.

Useful Vocabulary with /ʃ/	*Topics for Discussion*
interac**ti**on participa**ti**on discu**ssi**on	a. The interac**ti**on between the students and the professor in the classroom.
relation**sh**ip friend**sh**ip profe**ssi**onal	b. The relation**sh**ip between the students and the professor outside of the classroom.
tui**ti**on finan**ci**al scholar**sh**ips	c. Costs per year. Finan**ci**al aid.
admi**ssi**on competi**ti**on pre**ssu**re	d. Criteria for admi**ssi**on.

Consonant Four: /r/ as in *right* (vs. /l/)

1. The /r/ sound is spelled *r* (road) and *wr* (wrong).

2. Some students replace the /r/ with /l/ or /w/ so that *correct* sounds like *collect* or *rest* sounds like *west*. Other students omit the /r/ after vowels so that *heart* approximates *hot*. Finally, some students tap the tongue rapidly one or more times against the upper gum ridge to make /r/. This final tongue-tap variation is not likely to cause mis-understanding.

3. Some regional dialects of American English omit the /r/ after vowels (i.e., *pafk, afgue,* and *feaf*).

LISTENING ACTIVITY 1

Listen to the /r/ sound.

/r/ . . . /r/ . . . /r/ . . . /r/ . . . /r/

LISTENING ACTIVITY 2

Listen to the words with /r/. Do you hear the sound at the beginning (B), in the middle (M), or at the end (E) of each word? Close your books and write B, M, or E on a piece of paper. Check the *Answer Key.*

a. radio	e. arrive	i. however
b. rest	f. right	j. grew
c. here	g. history	k. brush
d. fair	h. around	l. room

LISTENING ACTIVITY 3

Listen to the word pairs. Which word of each pair has the /r/ sound—the first or the second? Close your books and write 1 or 2 on a piece of paper. Check the *Answer Key.*

a. crowd	cloud	f. run	one	k. rice	lice
b. wrong	long	g. went	rent	l. pot	part
c. lead	read	h. here	heel	m. lawn	learn
d. erect	elect	i. halt	heart	n. sharp	shop
e. right	light	j. stale	stare		

LISTENING ACTIVITY 4

Listen to the sentences with one of the words in parentheses. Mark the correct reponse/meaning. Check the *Answer Key.*

a. You have the (long, wrong) number.
_____ You need the short one.
_____ Hang up and dial again.

b. Where does she (pray, play)?
_____ At church.
_____ At the playground.

c. I watched the (clouds, crowds) go by.
_____ In the sky.
_____ In the street.

d. He looks like he's (bowling, boring).
_____ He's holding a ball.
_____ He has such a dull expression.

e. Would you (rake, wake) them up?
_____ Those leaves are killing the grass.
_____ They've been sleeping all morning.

f. What's your favorite (spot, sport) in the United States?
_____ I like the southwest.
_____ I like baseball.

LISTENING ACTIVITY 5

Listen to the paragraph. Fill in the blanks with words that have the /r/ sound. Check the *Answer Key*.

Butterflies in Your Stomach

If you've ever given a _____ in _____ of a class or a _____ of people, you know the feeling. Your _____ _____, your blood _____ _____, your hands _____ to shake, your _____ gets _____, and you get _____ flies in your stomach. What causes your body to _____ this way? When you're _____ or _____, your glands _____ adrenalin into your blood_____. The _____ causes your muscles to tense up. It also causes _____ motion in your stomach muscles. As a _____, your stomach _____ _____ acid than it needs for digestion. The acid feels like _____ flies in your stomach.

Figure B-5
Forming the voiced /r/ sound. The whole tongue is pulled up and back against the upper back teeth and hard palate as if you were saying /g/ as in *green*. Raise the tip of your tongue and curl it slightly toward the upper gum ridge (but don't touch the gum ridge). As you make the sound, your tongue tenses and your upper lip tenses and protrudes slightly.

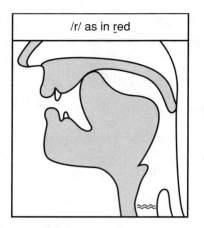

/r/ as in r̲ed

Note: When you make an /l/ sound, the tip of the tongue touches the upper gum ridge.

EXERCISE 1

Repeat the words with the /r/ sound.

write	hurry	her
result	hard	offer
repeat	experience	sir
radiation	married	fur
room	boring	beer
rude	different	year
routine	practice	share
robot	contract	four
rice	free	car

Note: When /r/ occurs after a vowel, sometimes the pronunciation is simply /ɜr/ as in *girl*. The /ɜr/ sound usually occurs in words spelled *-ir* (bird), *-er* (her), and *-ur* (turn).

EXERCISE 2

Words that contain both an /r/ and an /l/ might be especially difficult. Repeat these words:

frequently, really, rarely, clearly, early, realize, religion, learn, problem, electric, salary, large, celebrate, parallel

EXERCISE 3   Choose three words with /r/ that you use frequently. Write a typical phrase or sentence that you might say with each of the words. Practice each sentence three times.

a. _____

b. _____

c. _____

EXERCISE 4

Repeat the word pairs in Listening Activity 3. Make a clear distinction between /r/ and /l/ and between /r/ and /w/.

EXERCISE 5

Practice the italicized words silently. Repeat the sentences. Look up from your book as you say each sentence.

a. Turn **_right_** at the next light.

b. Some bumper **_stickers_** say, "**_Arrive_** alive!"

c. The **_calculator_** is **_solar-powered_**.

d. What's the **_price_** of a new set of **_tires_**?

e. **_Marketing_** meetings are held on **_Fridays_**.

f. They**_'re_** negotiating a new **_trade agreement_**.

g. Who's the **_principal investigator_** in the **_research project_**?

h. She was given a substantial **_raise_**.

j. I'll have to do one **_more revision_**.

EXERCISE 6   Record yourself reading the paragraph titled "Butterflies in Your Stomach" in Listening Activity 5 in the *Answer Key*. Monitor your pronunciation of words with /r/.

COMMUNICATIVE PRACTICE 1   In a group of three or four students, underline and preview the pronunciation of all of the menu items with an /r/.

Student 1 plays the role of the waiter/waitress and writes down what each customer wants. Student 1 has access to descriptions of the menu items on the page following the menu. The other students are customers and order complete meals. If the customers want explanations of the entrees, they should ask the waiter.

MENU

Entrees

Served with your choice of two vegetables, a garden salad with choice of dressing, and rolls

Pasta Primavera
Southern Fried Chicken
London Broil
Burritos

Baked Chicken Breast
Chicken Teriyaki
Crabmeat au Gratin
Sweet and Sour Shrimp

Today's Special

Broiled Haddock Fillets
Served with brown rice, fresh peas, and crusty French bread

Vegetables

French-fried potatoes
Sliced tomatoes with basil
Broccoli spears
Zucchini-carrot medley
Corn on the cob
French-style green beans

Beverages

Fresh brewed coffee
Tea—hot or iced
Assorted soft drinks
Milk
Fresh lemonade

Desserts

Fresh fruit sorbet
   Assorted flavors
Blueberry pie a la mode
Carrot cake
   Cream cheese frosting

Fresh strawberries
   In season
Ice cream sundae
   French vanilla topped with hot fudge sauce,
   nuts, whipped cream, and a cherry

Menu adapted from "Eating Better When Eating Out," U.S. Department of Agriculture, Home and Garden Bulletin No. 232-11.

INFORMATION FOR STUDENT 1 (WAITER)

Pasta Primavera
Ribbons of fettucini and fresh vegetables tossed in a yogurt sauce, sprinkled with Parmesan cheese

Southern Fried Chicken
Fried to a crispy golden brown

London Broil
Grilled strips of flank steak served with fresh mushrooms; cooked to order

Burritos
Your choice of beef, chicken, or bean; served with rice and fresh salsa

Choice of Salad Dressings:
House Dressing—Vinaigrette
Ranch
Blue Cheese
French
Thousand Island

Baked Chicken Breast
Boneless breast of chicken baked in a delicate lemon-basil sauce

Chicken Teriyaki
Grilled strips of chicken marinated in spicy teriyaki sauce

Crabmeat au Gratin
Crabmeat in a creamy cheese sauce, baked to a delicate brown

Sweet and Sour Shrimp
Batter-fried shrimp covered with a tangy sweet and sour sauce

Consonant Five: /v/ as in *vote* (vs. /w/, /b/, and /f/)

1. Some students replace the /v/ with a /w/ and vice-versa so that *veal* sounds like *wheel* and *while* sounds like *vile*. Other students replace the /v/ with a /b/ so that *very* sounds like *berry*. Still other students replace the voiced /v/ with the voiceless /f/ so that *have* sounds like *half*.

LISTENING ACTIVITY 1

Listen to the /v/ sound.

/v/ . . . /v/ . . . /v/ . . . /v/ . . . /v/

LISTENING ACTIVITY 2

Listen to the words with /v/. Do you hear the /v/ sound at the beginning (B), in the middle (M), or at the end (E) of each word? Close your books and write B, M, or E on a piece of paper. Check the *Answer Key*.

a. visit	f. heavy
b. video	g. novel
c. develop	h. value
d. twelve	i. save
e. vote	j. level

LISTENING ACTIVITY 3

Listen to the word pairs. Which word of each pair has the /v/ sound— the first or the second? Close your books and write 1 or 2 on a piece of paper. Check the *Answer Key*.

a. very	wary	h. very	berry
b. vie	why	i. volt	bolt
c. west	vest	j. boats	votes
d. veil	whale	k. ban	van
e. wheel	veal	l. leaf	leave
f. verse	worse	m. have	half
g. evoke	awoke	n. lover	lower

LISTENING ACTIVITY 4

Listen to the sentences with one of the words in parentheses. Mark the correct response/meaning. Check the *Answer Key.*

a. Where did you put the (veal, wheel)?
_____ In the freezer.
_____ On the bike.

b. What kind of (vine, wine) did you get?
_____ A dry, red wine.
_____ One with blue flowers.

c. They (evoke, awoke) her.
_____ They remind me of her.
_____ They didn't want her to oversleep.

d. What happened with the (vote, boat)?
_____ Our candidate won.
_____ The engine died.

e. He's (serving, surfing) in Hawaii.
_____ He's been in the navy for over two years.
_____ He loves to ride the waves.

LISTENING ACTIVITY 5

Listen to the paragraph. Fill in the blanks with words that have the /v/ sound. Check the *Answer Key.*

Valentine's Day*

For _____ 100 years, it has been popular to _____ cards, flowers, gifts and other tokens of _____ on February 14, St. _____ Day in the United States. There are _____ explanations for the origin of this holiday; _____, the most _____ is that St. _____ Day is a _____ of a February 15 Roman _____. During this _____, bachelors picked names of women to _____ who their "_____" or _____ would be for the coming year. The couples then exchanged gifts and sometimes _____ became engaged.

*Source: *World Book Encyclopedia,* Chicago: World Book, Inc., Vol. 20, 1992, p. 277.

Figure B-6
Forming the voiced /v/ sound. Lightly touch the upper teeth to the inside of the lower lip. Use your vocal cords.

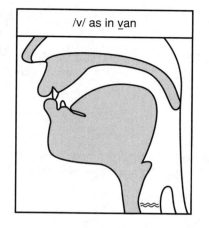

/v/ as in <u>v</u>an

EXERCISE 1

Repeat the words with /v/.

video	never	leave
valid	invest	save
victim	divide	above
vice-president	develop	alive
velocity	seven	improve
vacation	movie	arrive
vegetables	advice	active
visit	heavy	you've

EXERCISE 2

Words that contain both a /v/ and /w/, /b/, or /f/ might be especially difficult. Repeat these words.

With /w/	*With /b/*	*With /f/*
vowel	behavior	forgive
wives	vibration	favor
we've	believe	fever

EXERCISE 3 Choose three words with /v/ that you use frequently. Write a typical phrase or sentence you might say with each of the words. Practice each sentence three times.

a. _____

b. _____

c. _____

EXERCISE 4

Repeat the word pairs in Listening Activity 3. Make a clear distinction between /v/ and /w/, /v/ and /b/, and /v/ and /f/.

EXERCISE 5

Practice blending the final /v/ with the first sound of the next word in the phrases below. Repeat the phrases. Say each phrase as if it were one word.

leave_valuables	save_victims
leave_friends	save_books
leave_home	save_text
leave_together	save_money
leave_alone	save_information

EXERCISE 6

Practice the italicized words silently. Repeat the sentences. Look up from the book as you say each sentence.

a. Would you do me a **favor**?

b. Where did you go on your **vacation**?

c. Which **movie** did you see?

d. What kind of **advice** did she *give* you?

e. Should I **save** it or *invest* it?

f. After **twelve** years of marriage, they got a **divorce**.

g. I'd like to *invite* you to my **anniversary** party.

h. When can we **leave**?

i. His **fever** got worse and worse.

Now circle the words above that begin with a /w/ sound.

Repeat the sentences again and monitor for /w/.

EXERCISE 7

Record yourself reading the paragraph titled "Valentine's Day" in Listening Activity 5 in the *Answer Key*. Monitor the italicized words with /v/.

COMMUNICATIVE PRACTICE

In a group of three to five students, discuss vacation time in your countries. Monitor for the /v/ sound in the key vocabulary listed below. Be careful to use /w/, not /v/, in these words: worker, white-collar, one, and week. Report the highlights of your group's discussion to the class.

Useful Vocabulary with /v/	*Topics for Discussion*
vary have average	1. How long is the average vacation for blue-collar workers in your country?
seven every vacation five	2. How long is the average vacation for white-collar workers in your country?
service	3. What is the relationship between length of service in a company and length of vacation?
deserve government	4. Do workers in your country usually take all of the vacation that they deserve? Are there any laws in your country regarding vacation time?
travel visit overseas drive	5. How do people in your country like to spend their vacations?

Vowels
· · · · · · · ·

An Overview of the Vowel Sounds of American English

The vowel sounds of American English are represented below with phonetic symbols used in the *Longman Dictionary of American English* (1983) and with key words representing some of the various spelling patterns for each sound.

Front Vowels

Front vowels are made with the **front** of the tongue arched. Beginning with the first front vowel /iʸ/, the front part of the tongue is high in the mouth. The tongue and jaw drop lower and lower as you move down the list of front vowels. Front vowels are also made with the lips spread in varying degrees.

Repeat the sounds and the key words after your teacher or the speaker on the tape:

1. /iʸ/   h**e**, s**ee**, f**ee**t, m**ea**t   4. /ɛ/   m**e**t, l**e**t, d**ea**d

2. /ɪ/   h**i**t, **i**f, p**i**ck   5. /æ/   m**a**d, **a**sk, c**a**sh

3. /eʸ/   m**ay**, **A**sia, f**a**c**e**, p**ai**n

Figure C-1
The tongue positions for front vowels

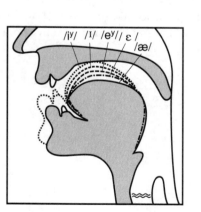

Central Vowels

Central vowels are made with the **middle** of the tongue slightly arched. The tongue and jaw are higher for /ʌ/ and /ə/ than for /ɑ/. The lips are neither spread nor rounded for central vowels.

Repeat the sounds and key words after your teacher or the speaker on the tape.

6. /ɜr/   g*ir*l, h*er*, t*ur*n

7. /ʌ/   n*u*t, *u*p, d*u*mb

    /ə/   *a*bout, c*o*ncern

(Vowel sound 7 has two symbols. The first symbol /ʌ/ is used in **stressed** words and syllables like c*u*t and *u*nder and the second symbol /ə/ is used in **unstressed** words and syllables like w*a*s and *a*lone.)

8. /ɑ/   n*o*t, b*o*ss, c*o*ncert, f*a*ther

Figure C-2

The tongue positions for central vowels

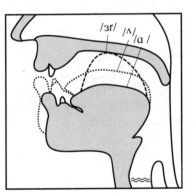

Back Vowels

Back vowels are made with the **back** part of the tongue arched. Beginning with the first back vowel /uʷ/, the back part of the tongue is high. The tongue and jaw drop lower and lower as you move down the list of back vowels. Back vowels are also made with the lips rounded in varying degrees.

 Repeat the sounds and the key words after your teacher or the speaker on the tape.

9. /uʷ/   *too, food, rude, flew, juice*

10. /ʊ/   *took, foot, should, put*

11. /oʷ/   *no, low, hope, loan, okay*

12. /ɔ/   *law, cause, born*

(Some speakers of American English do not distinguish between vowel 8, /ɑ/ as in c**o**t, and vowel 12, /ɔ/ as in c**au**ght.)

Figure C-3
The tongue positions for back vowels

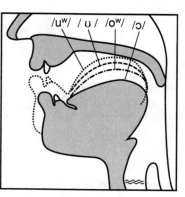

Diphthongs

Diphthongs are combinations of two vowel sounds. Your mouth moves and changes shape as you pronounce diphthongs.

 Repeat the three diphthongs and the key words after your teacher or the speaker on the tape.

13. /aɪ/   *tie, like, by*

14. /aʊ/   *out, loud, now*

15. /ɔɪ/   *toy, voice*

The Vowel Chart

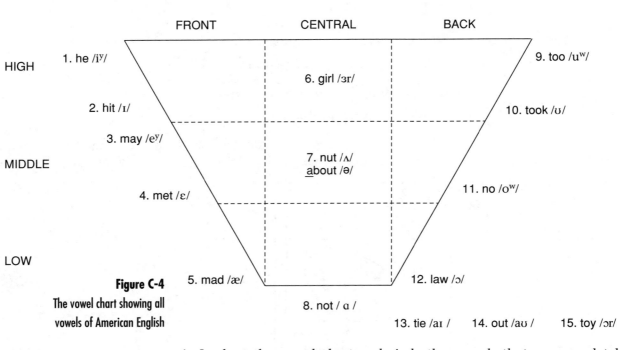

Figure C-4
The vowel chart showing all vowels of American English

1. Look at the vowel chart and circle the sounds that are completely different from those in your native language.

2. Refer to your *Speech Profile Summary Form* in Chapter 1. Which vowel sounds did your teacher indicate were troublesome for you? List them below.

_____   _____   _____

3. Are there any other vowel sounds that are difficult for you? List them below.

_____   _____   _____

Tense and Lax Vowels

The vowels /iʸ/ (he), /eʸ/ (made), /uʷ/ (too), and /oʷ/ (no) are pronounced with muscle tension. They are longer in duration and sometimes easier for learners of English to hear and to say. The remaining vowels are shorter in duration and are made with the muscles in a more relaxed (lax) position.

Repeat the following tense/lax vowel pairs. Notice the face, lip, and tongue muscles tense and relax.

Tense	Lax
/iʸ/ he	/ɪ/ hit
/eʸ/ made	/ɛ/ met
/uʷ/ too	/ʊ/ took
/oʷ/ no	/ɔ/ law

The tense vowels are not pure vowels. Instead, they move from one vowel sound toward a second vowel sound. Your mouth has to move and change shape in order to pronounce these vowels correctly.

Repeat the above pairs again. Notice the movement in the direction of a second sound in the tense vowels.

Vowel Practices

This section provides concentrated practice with vowel sounds that are especially troublesome for intermediate to advanced speakers of English. Five vowel sounds are reviewed and contrasted with sounds many learners of English use as replacements. These include the following:

1. Vowel 2: /ɪ/ as in *hit* (vs. /iʸ/ as in *he*)

2. Vowel 4: /ɛ/ as in *met* (vs. /eʸ/ as in *made*; /æ/ as in *mad*)

3. Vowel 7: /ʌ/ as in *nut* (vs. /ɑ/ as in *not*)

4. Vowel 10: /ʊ/ as in *took* (vs. /uʷ/ as in *too*)

5. Vowel 8: /ɑ/ as in *not* (vs. /oʷ/ as in *no*)

Each vowel review includes a *Listen* and an *Exercise* section for independent laboratory use, as well as a *Communicative Practice* section for follow-up classroom practice in pairs and small groups. The *Answer Key* for Appendix C is at the end of the text.

As you work on vowel pronunciation, notice that vowel sound/spelling patterns are more varied and unpredictable than consonant sound/spelling patterns. Also, notice that it is harder to see and feel the tongue position for vowel sounds than for consonant sounds. As a result, you might need to rely more on listening to make judgments about accuracy.

If you are having difficulty with vowel sounds not included here, ask your teacher to recommend a textbook that presents a survey of all speech sounds.

1. Vowel 2: /ɪ/ as in *hit* (vs. Vowel 1: /iʸ/ as in *he*)

1. The /ɪ/ is a pure vowel; it is short in duration. The /iʸ/ is longer in duration and glides upward toward a /y/ sound.

2. Many students confuse /iʸ/ for /ɪ/ and vice-versa so that *fit* sounds like *feet* and *eat* sounds like *it*.

LISTENING ACTIVITY 1

Listen to /ɪ/.

/ɪ/ . . . /ɪ/ . . . /ɪ/ . . . /ɪ/ . . .

Now listen to /ɪ/ contrasted with /iʸ/.

/ɪ/ . . . /iʸ/ . . . /ɪ/ . . . /iʸ/ . . . /ɪ/ . . . /iʸ/

LISTENING ACTIVITY 2

Listen to the words with /ɪ/.

h*i*t, d*i*sk, d*i*d, g*i*ve, w*i*th, m*i*ss, *i*nch, w*i*sh, c*i*ty, m*i*nute, l*i*ve, cons*i*der, v*i*sit

---

LISTENING ACTIVITY 3

Listen to the word pairs. Which word in each pair has the /ɪ/ sound—the first or second? Close your books and write 1 or 2 on a separate piece of paper. Check the *Answer Key.*

a.	hit	heat	f. live	leave
b.	it	eat	g. seen	sin
c.	heel	hill	h. list	least
d.	deed	did	i. will	wheel
e.	feet	fit	j. sleep	slip

LISTENING ACTIVITY 4

Listen to the sentences with one of the words in parentheses. Mark the correct meaning/response. Check the *Answer Key.*

1. Did you (slip, sleep)?

   _____Yes, on the ice.

   _____Yes, for ten hours.

2. Those were beautiful (pitches, peaches).

_____It was a great baseball game.

_____It was a good crop.

3. Is the patient going to (live, leave)?

_____Yes. Her injuries weren't serious.

_____Yes. She's packing her bags now.

4. Did you (hit, heat) it?

_____Yes, with the hammer.

_____Yes, in the microwave.

5. Where should I put the (pills, peels)?

_____In the medicine chest.

_____In the garbage.

LISTENING ACTIVITY 5

Listen to the following paragraph. Fill in the blanks with the words that have the /ɪ/ sound in stressed words and syllables. Check the *Answer Key.*

Drinking and Health Risks*

People often _____ a glass to toast good health.

_____ may indeed lower the _____

of several diseases, according to some _____

_____ released by the Harvard School of Public Health.

Researchers found that up to one to two _____ each day

_____ the _____ of heart attack, stroke,

and fatal heart disease by about _____ percent in men

and up to _____ percent in _____. One

researcher warned, however, that _____ with a family

_____ of breast cancer should _____

_____ since alcohol is _____ to a higher

_____ of breast cancer.

*Source: Beth Weinhouse, "Your Health," *Redbook*, January 1992, p. 19.

EXERCISE 1

Repeat the words with /ɪ/.

*i*f	h*i*t
*i*ll	f*i*t
*i*nto	l*i*ve
*i*ncrease, n.	s*i*t
*i*mage	l*i*st
*i*ncidence	w*i*n
*i*nnocent	cons*i*der
*i*nterstate	b*u*siness

EXERCISE 2

Choose three words with /ɪ/ that you use frequently. Write typical sentences you might say with the words. Practice each sentence three times.

a. _____

b. _____

c. _____

EXERCISE 3

Repeat the word pairs in Listening Activity 3. Make a clear distinction between /ɪ/ and /iʸ/.

EXERCISE 4

Practice the italicized words silently. Repeat the sentences. Look up from your book as you say each sentence.

a. Dollar **bills** usually wear out in less than two years.

b. My dentist found **six** cavities.

c. He's five feet nine **inches** tall.

d. Put the **fish** and **chicken** in the freezer.

e. What's your favorite **city** to *visit*?

f. I **live** in the **fifth** house on the right.

g. Did she **fix** the **printer**?

h. What's your **opinion**?

EXERCISE 5 Record yourself reading the paragraph titled "Drinking and Health Risks" in Listening Activity 5 in the *Answer Key*. Monitor your pronunciation of the italicized words with /ɪ/.

COMMUNICATIVE PRACTICE Practice the /ɪ/ sound as you create a "Wish List." Pick the five items which, in your opinion, would most improve the quality of life. Number the five items in order of importance. Feel free to add additional items to the list.

In small groups of four to six students, discuss the items most important to you and justify your choices. Try to reach consensus with your group on the top two items.

Practice and monitor the words with /ɪ/ that are likely to occur during the discussion: if, think, wish, opinion, pick, list, important, individual, improve, and fifth.

WISH LIST

Individual	*Group*	
_____	_____	Quality education for everyone
_____	_____	More free time
_____	_____	Drug-free world
_____	_____	Human colonies in space
_____	_____	Personal robots
_____	_____	End to prejudice
_____	_____	Housing for the homeless
_____	_____	Cures for deadly diseases
_____	_____	Adequate health care for everyone
_____	_____	Living in crime-free cities
_____	_____	More time with family
_____	_____	World peace
_____	_____	Full employment
_____	_____	End to hunger
_____	_____	Nonpolluting energy sources
_____	_____	_____
_____	_____	_____

2. Vowel 4: /ɛ/ as in *met* (vs. Vowel 3: /eʸ/ as in *made;* and Vowel 5: /æ/ as in *mad*)

1. The /ɛ/ and /æ/ are pure vowels; they are short in duration. The /eʸ/ is longer in duration and glides upward toward a /y/ sound.

2. Many students replace the /ɛ/ with /eʸ/ and vice-versa so that *let* sounds like *late* and *paper* sounds like *pepper*. Other students may use an approximation of the /ɛ/ for the /æ/ sound so that *bad* sounds like *bed*.

LISTENING ACTIVITY 1

Listen to /ɛ/.

/ɛ/ . . . /ɛ/ . . . /ɛ/ . . . /ɛ/ . . . /ɛ/

Now listen to the contrast between /ɛ/ and /eʸ/.

/ɛ/ . . . /eʸ/ . . . /ɛ/ . . . /eʸ/ . . . /ɛ/ . . . /eʸ/

LISTENING ACTIVITY 2

Listen to the words with /ɛ/.

let, yes, end, dead, met, left, guess, better, never, chemistry, effective

---
LISTENING ACTIVITY 3

Listen to the word pairs. Does the first or the second word in each pair have the /ɛ/ sound? Close your books and write 1 or 2 on a separate piece of paper. Check the *Answer Key.*

a.	late	let	e.	taste	test	h.	later	letter
b.	date	debt	f.	men	main	i.	guess	gas
c.	edge	age	g.	fell	fail	j.	men	man
d.	wet	wait						

LISTENING ACTIVITY 4

Listen to each sentence with one of the words in parentheses. Mark the correct meaning/response. Check the *Answer Key.*

1. Could you buy some black (pepper, paper) for me?

   _____ For dinner tonight.

   _____ For my art project.

2. He just (left, laughed).

    _____ I'm sorry you missed him.

    _____ He thought it was funny.

3. How did you like the (test, taste)?

    _____ It was hard.

    _____ It was too spicy.

4. I met the (men, man) you work with.

    _____ Did you like them?

    _____ Did you like him?

5. It's the right (edge, age).

    _____ Nice and sharp.

    _____ Not too old and not too young.

LISTENING ACTIVITY 5

Listen to the following paragraph. Fill in the blanks with words that have the /ɛ/ sound in stressed words and syllables. Check the *Answer Key.*

Airbags

The airbag has become standard equipment in new cars. It is stored in the _____ of the steering wheel, and, in an accident, quickly inflates to _____ save a driver's life. The airbag has electronic _____ that can feel a crash as it begins to happen. The _____ _____ off a small can of nitrogen gas, which rushes into the bag. The soft bag _____ the driver and _____ it deflates. Airbags are only useful in _____-on or rear- _____ accidents. During a side collision, a driver needs a seat_____ for _____.

EXERCISE 1

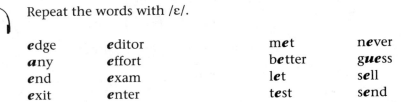

Repeat the words with /ɛ/.

edge	**e**ditor	m**e**t	n**e**ver
any	**e**ffort	b**e**tter	g**ue**ss
end	**e**xam	l**e**t	s**e**ll
exit	**e**nter	t**e**st	s**e**nd

EXERCISE 2

Choose three words with /ɛ/ that you use frequently. Write typical sentences you might say with the words. Practice each sentence three times.

a. _____

b. _____

c. _____

EXERCISE 3

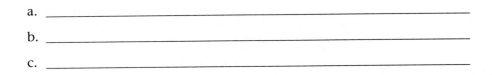

Repeat the word pairs in Listening Activity 3. Make a clear distinction between /ɛ/ and /eʸ/ and between /ɛ/ and /æ/.

EXERCISE 4

Practice the italicized words silently. Repeat the sentences. Look up from your book as you say the sentences.

a. My ***relatives left yesterday.***

b. That was an ***excellent question.***

c. Did you ***forget*** to ***send*** the ***letter***?

d. The ***presidential election*** is ***next November.***

e. My ***best friend sent*** me this ***present.***

f. I've ***already spent everything*** that you ***lent*** to me.

g. Take the ***elevator*** to the ***second*** floor.

h. The ***recipe*** calls for a teaspoon of black ***pepper.***

EXERCISE 5

Record yourself reading the paragraph titled "Airbags" in Listening Activity 5 in the *Answer Key*. Monitor your pronunciation of the italicized words with /ɛ/.

COMMUNICATIVE PRACTICE   Work in pairs to create a graph depicting temperatures around the world. Student 1 has an incomplete temperature chart below. Student 2 has an incomplete chart on the following page. Without looking at each other's charts, obtain the missing information from your partner.

WORLD WEATHER FOR NOVEMBER

City	Temperature Range in Fahrenheit Degrees
_____	53–66
Beijing	28–48
Budapest	33–47
Cairo	57–__
_____	53–84
Hong Kong	65–74
_____	46–__
Miami	66–__
Moscow	26–35
San Juan	__–__
Tokyo	43–60

WORLD WEATHER FOR NOVEMBER*

City	Temperature Range in Fahrenheit Degrees
Athens	53–66
Beijing	__–48
_____	33–__
Cairo	__–77
Delhi	53–84
Hong Kong	__–__
Mexico City	46–67
_____	66–77
Moscow	__–35
_____	77–84
Tokyo	43–60

Then with your partner create a graph that clearly shows the temperature differences among the cities listed. Where would you most like to visit and least like to visit during the month of November?

Practice and monitor words with /ɛ/ that are likely to recur: November, weather, temperature, seventy, seven, Mexico, and twenty. Be sure to use the /eʸ/, not /ɛ/, in these words: range, eight, and eighty.

*Source: Conway, McKinley, and Linda L. Liston (eds.), *The Weather Handbook,* Atlanta: Conway Data, Inc., 1990, 355–502.

3. Vowel 7: /ʌ/ as in *nut* (vs. Vowel 8: /ɑ/ as in *not*)

1. The /ʌ/ is a central vowel. It is neutral because in producing the vowel sound the tongue and jaw are relaxed and the lips are neither rounded nor spread.

2. Many students replace /ʌ/ with /ɑ/ and vice versa so that *luck* sounds like *lock* and *shot* sounds like *shut*.

LISTENING ACTIVITY 1

Listen to the /ʌ/ sound.

/ʌ/ . . . /ʌ/ . . . /ʌ/ . . . /ʌ/ . . . /ʌ/

Listen to /ʌ/ contrasted with /ɑ/.
/ʌ/ . . . /ɑ/ . . . /ʌ/ . . . /ɑ/ . . . /ʌ/ . . . /ɑ/

LISTENING ACTIVITY 2

Listen to the words with /ʌ/.

up, b**u**t, f**u**n, c**u**t, l**u**ck, **u**nder, **u**gly, s**u**pper, st**u**dy, p**u**blic, l**o**ve, c**o**me, m**o**ney

---
LISTENING ACTIVITY 3

Listen to the word pairs. Does the first or the second word in each pair have the /ʌ/ sound? Close your books and write 1 or 2 on a separate piece of paper. Check the *Answer Key*.

a.	bomb	bum	f.	wander	wonder
b.	robber	rubber	g.	color	collar
c.	come	calm	h.	duck	dock
d.	fund	fond	i.	boss	bus
e.	shut	shot	j.	stuck	stock

LISTENING ACTIVITY 4

Listen to each of the sentences with one of the words in parentheses. Mark the correct meaning/response. Check the *Answer Key*.

a. Is that a (duck, dog)?

_____ Yes. It has feathers.

_____ Yes. It has fur.

b. I need a (cup, cop).

_____ For coffee.

_____ For protection.

c. What an ugly (collar, color)!

_____ I hate buttons on collars.

_____ I hate that shade of green.

d. This is a hard (nut, knot).

_____ I can't crack it.

_____ I can't untie it.

e. Was your (luck, lock) good?

_____ No. I lost.

_____ No. It broke.

LISTENING ACTIVITY 5

Listen to the following paragraph. Fill in the blanks with words that have the /ʌ/ sound in stressed words and syllables. Check the *Answer Key.*

Foreign Student Numbers Are Up*

During the 1990–199 ___ academic year, foreign students _____ in U.S. colleges and universities _____ to an all-time high of _____,500. This _____ represents an increase of 5.3% over the previous year. Asian students accounted for 40% of the total and _____ of the growth. In fact, Japanese student enrollment _____ in the previous three academic years. Substantial increases were noted from Europe as well. The _____ of students _____ from Eastern European _____ was _____ 42% over the previous year.

*Source: *ESL-HEIS Newsletter*, "Foreign Student Enrollment in US Higher Education Exceeds 400,000," Jan.–Feb. 1991, p. 4.

EXERCISE 1

Repeat the words with /ʌ/.

up	b**u**s
under	j**u**st
ugly	s**u**n
umpire	l**u**nch
uncle	l**u**ck
ulcer	m**o**ney
ultimate	s**o**mebody
upkeep	c**o**lor

EXERCISE 2   Choose three words with /ʌ/ that you use frequently. Write typical sentences that you might say with the words. Practice each sentence three times.

a. _____

b. _____

c. _____

EXERCISE 3

Repeat the word pairs in Listening Activity 3. Make a clear distinction between /ʌ/ and /ɑ/.

EXERCISE 4

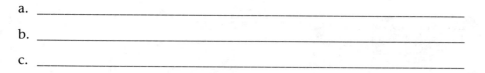

Practice the italicized words silently. Repeat the sentences. Look up from your book as you say each sentence.

a. Let's ***discuss*** your ***assumptions.***

b. Do you have ***enough money*** for ***lunch***?

c. Are you going to ***study*** during ***summer*** quarter?

d. We have ***another*** meeting on ***Monday***?

e. I ***wonder*** what we're having for ***supper.***

f. The ***customer*** ordered a ***dozen*** roses.

g. He presented his ***results*** in his ***introduction.***

h. *x* is a ***function*** of *y*.

EXERCISE 5   Record yourself reading the paragraph titled "Foreign Student Numbers Are Up" in Listening Activity 5 in the *Answer Key.* Monitor your pronunciation of the italicized words with /ʌ/.

COMMUNICATIVE PRACTICE   In small groups of two or three students, attempt to decode the brain-teasers or puzzles below. Interpret each message to create an English word or phrase.

     Which answers have the /ʌ/ sound and which ones have the /ɑ/ sound? Check the *Answer Key.**

Example

R
R O A D   Answer: CROSSROADS (cr**o**ssroads = /ɑ/)
A
D

1. WEAR
   LONG

2.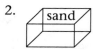

3. i   i
   ○ ○
   ○ ○
   ○ ○

4. T
    O
    U
    C
    H

5. GROUND

6. KNEE
   LIGHTS

7. TROUBLE
   TROUBLE

*Adapted from John W. Newstrom and James E. Scannel. *Games Trainers Play*. New York: McGraw-Hill, 1980, pp. 75 and 77. Used with permission.

4. Vowel 10: /ʊ/ as in *took* (vs. Vowel 9: /uʷ/ as in *too*)

1. The /ʊ/ is a pure vowel and is short in duration. The /uʷ/ is longer in duration and glides toward a /w/ sound.

2. Many students confuse /uʷ/ for /ʊ/ so that *pull* sounds like *pool* and *fool* sounds like *full*. Some students also replace the /ʊ/ with /ʌ/ so that *look* sounds like *luck*.

LISTENING ACTIVITY 1

Listen to /ʊ/.

/ʊ/ . . . /ʊ/ . . . /ʊ/ . . . /ʊ/ . . . /ʊ/

Now listen to /ʊ/ contrasted with /uʷ/.

/ʊ/ . . . /uʷ/ . . . /ʊ/ . . . /uʷ/ . . . /ʊ/ . . . /uʷ/.

LISTENING ACTIVITY 2

Listen to words with /ʊ/.

l**oo**k, t**oo**k, c**oo**k, f**oo**t, g**oo**d, p**u**t, f**u**ll, sh**ou**ld, w**ou**ldn't, b**oo**kcase, underst**oo**d

---

LISTENING ACTIVITY 3

Listen to the word pairs. Does the first or second word in each pair have the /ʊ/ sound? Close your books and write 1 or 2 on a separate piece of paper. Check the *Answer Key*.

a. should   shooed   e. who'd   hood
b. pool   pull   f. look   luck
c. fool   full   g. took   tuck
d. stood   stewed   h. cud   could

LISTENING ACTIVITY 4

Listen to each of the sentences with one of the words in parentheses. Mark the correct meaning/response. Check the *Answer Key*.

a. Can you clean this black (soot, suit) right away?

_____ It's all over the fireplace.

_____ I need to wear it this afternoon.

b. He has no more (pull, pool).

_____ He's lost all of his influence.

_____ He'll have to swim somewhere else.

c. We can't eat until the meat has (stood, stewed) for an hour.

_____ It needs to cool.

_____ It needs to be tender.

d. They (took, tuck) their shirts in.

_____ To the cleaners.

_____ To their pants.

LISTENING ACTIVITY 5

Listen to the following paragraph. Fill in the blanks with words that have the /ʊ/ sound in stressed words or syllables. Check the *Answer Key*.

Eating Out

People in the United States are spending less time

_____ and more time eating out in restaurants. In fact, many people in the United States eat out on the average of four times a week. If you invite someone to join you for dinner in a restaurant, here are some general guidelines. You _____ phone first in order to find out whether you need a reservation. When you invite someone to dinner, you _____ be prepared to pay the bill. However, sometimes the guests _____ rather pay so that they won't feel indebted to you. When the bill arrives, _____ to see if the tip has been added to the cost of the food. Most restaurants do not add the tip to the bill. You _____ leave a tip equal to 15% of the bill if the service was adequate. If the restaurant is expensive or if the service was especially _____, you _____ leave up to 20% of the bill.

EXERCISE 1

Repeat the words with /ʊ/.

push   understood
pull   good-bye
full   would
took   could
cook   should
foot

EXERCISE 2

Choose three words with /ʊ/ that you use frequently. Write typical sentences you might say with the words. Practice each sentence three times.

a. _____

b. _____

c. _____

EXERCISE 3

Repeat the word pairs in Listening Activity 3. Make a clear distinction between /ʊ/ and /uʷ/ and between /ʊ/ and /ʌ/.

EXERCISE 4

Practice the italicized words silently. Repeat the sentences. Look up from your book as you say each sentence.

a. I ***couldn't*** afford to buy the car.

b. We ***should*** apologize for the error.

c. ***Would*** you mind if I came late?

d. I ***would*** rather eat out than ***cook.***

e. He ***should*** have been more careful.

f. I don't remember where I ***put*** my ***books.***

g. The ***football*** stadium is ***full.***

h. The candidate promised to ***push*** for tax reforms.

EXERCISE 5

Record yourself reading the paragraph titled "Eating Out" in Listening Activity 5 in the *Answer Key.* Monitor your pronunciation of underlined words with /ʊ/.

You are part of a group of four to six anthropologists. You have been asked to select seven items that represent popular culture today. These items will be placed in a time capsule to give people of the next century an idea of what life was like today.

Preview the phrases with /ʊ/ that are likely to occur during your discussion:

I think we ***should*** . . .
We ***could*** . . .
We need to include a ***book*** . . .
We ought to ***put*** . . .
That ***would***(n't) be a ***good*** choice . . .

Here are some suggestions to get you started:

Laptop computer
Microwave oven
Recycled paper product
Low-fat frozen yogurt container
Sweatsuit

5. Vowel 8: /ɑ/ as in *not* (vs. Vowel 11: /oʷ/ as in *no*)

1. The /ɑ/ is a pure vowel. The /oʷ/ glides upward toward a /w/ sound.

2. Students sometimes confuse /oʷ/ for /ɑ/ so that *rob* sounds like *robe* and *hope* sounds like *hop*.

LISTENING ACTIVITY 1

Listen to the /ɑ/ sound.

/ɑ/ . . . /ɑ/ . . . /ɑ/ . . . /ɑ/ . . . /ɑ/

Listen to /ɑ/ contrasted with /oʷ/.

/ɑ/ . . . /oʷ/ . . . /ɑ/ . . . /oʷ/ . . . /ɑ/ . . . /oʷ/.

LISTENING ACTIVITY 2

Listen to the words with /ɑ/.

on, **o**ffer, j**o**b, n**o**t, sh**o**p, st**o**p, h**o**t, c**o**nduct, s**o**lid, b**o**ttom, w**a**llet, f**a**ther

---

LISTENING ACTIVITY 3

Listen to the word pairs. Does the first or second word in each pair have the /ɑ/ sound? Close your books and write 1 or 2 on a separate piece of paper. Check the *Answer Key.*

a.	not	note	f. odd	ode
b.	cot	coat	g. soak	sock
c.	stock	stoke	h. stoke	stock
d.	cope	cop	i. con	cone
e.	rob	robe	j. wrote	rot

LISTENING ACTIVITY 4

Listen to the sentences with one of the words in parentheses. Mark the correct meaning/response. Check the *Answer Key.*

a. He has a (scar, score).

_____ From the accident.

_____ From the game.

b. Tell (John, Joan) it's snowing.

_____ He'll be excited.

_____ She'll be excited.

c. Did you take care of the (knots, notes)?

_____ Yes. I untied them.

_____ Yes. I mailed them.

d. Did you get the (cod, code)?

_____ No. The market's out of fish.

_____ No. The programmer's still working on it.

LISTENING ACTIVITY 5

Listen to the paragraph. Fill in the blanks with words that have the /ɑ/ sound in stressed words and syllables. Check the *Answer Key*.

Jobs and Hormones

Testosterone, the hormone _____ for sex drive

and aggression, may have some influence on our choice of

_____. According to a recent study by a Georgia State

University _____ professor, people with high levels of

testosterone _____ for professions in which they face

severe competition in order to succeed. Actors have the most

testosterone of all; _____ and trial lawyers rank high

also. The lowest levels of testosterone are found among nurses and

ministers who devote themselves to comforting, not competing with,

others. Since women have lower levels of testosterone than men

in general, the researcher _____ that success is

_____ dependent on hormones. _____

is important, but it is _____ destiny.

EXERCISE 1   Repeat the words with /ɑ/.

on	c**o**st
odd	d**o**g
off	st**o**p
offer	sh**o**p
opposite	c**o**nfident
option	pr**o**bably
operate	f**o**llow
office	pr**o**duct

EXERCISE 2   Choose three words with /ɑ/ that you use frequently. Write typical sentences you might say with the words. Practice each sentence three times.

a. _____

b. _____

c. _____

EXERCISE 3

Repeat the word pairs in Listening Activity 3. Make a clear distinction between /ɑ/ and /oʷ/.

EXERCISE 4

Practice the italicized words silently. Repeat the sentences. Look up from your book as you say each sentence.

a. Which one *costs* the most?

b. *John* is doing his research in *robotics.*

c. The police *officer* caught the suspected *robber.*

d. There is a *lot* of *controversy* about *economic* recovery.

e. He *lost* a fortune in the *stock* market.

f. He's interested in *quality* control.

g. I'll *probably drop* it *off* on the way home.

h. The temperature should remain *constant.*

EXERCISE 5   Record yourself reading the paragraph titled "Jobs and Hormones" in Listening Activity 5 in the *Answer Key.* Monitor your pronunciation of the italicized words with /ɑ/.

COMMUNICATIVE PRACTICE   What is important in a job? What motivates employees? Each student should rate the following criteria contributing to job satisfaction on a scale of 1–5. Then select the three most important factors and the three least important factors.

In groups of three to five students, compare your answers. Was there agreement on any of the criteria? What might account for differences of opinion? Did you rank the items from the perspective of an employee or a boss?

Preview words with /ɑ/ that are likely to occur during the discussion: job, problems, opportunity, possibility, office, not, long, boss, cooperative. Monitor /oʷ/ in these words: most, promotion, and motivate.

FACTORS CONTRIBUTING TO JOB SATISFACTION

How important are these factors?

	1 = extremely important;	2 = important;	3 = slightly important;	4 = not important at all
High Pay	1	2	3	4
Job Security	1	2	3	4
Group Health Insurance	1	2	3	4
Possibility for Promotion	1	2	3	4
Opportunity to Improve Skills	1	2	3	4
Good Working Conditions	1	2	3	4
Interesting Work	1	2	3	4
Support from Boss	1	2	3	4
Appreciation of Work Done	1	2	3	4
Help with Personal Problems	1	2	3	4
Participation in Decision Making	1	2	3	4
Day-Care Service	1	2	3	4
Flexible Hours	1	2	3	4
Long Paid Vacations	1	2	3	4
Being Your Own Boss	1	2	3	4
Working Alone	1	2	3	4
Cooperative Co-workers	1	2	3	4
Distance from Home	1	2	3	4

List the Three Most Important Factors

1. _____

2. _____

3. _____

List the Three Least Important Factors

1. _____

2. _____

3. _____

Answer Key for Appendix B

Voiced and Voiceless Consonants

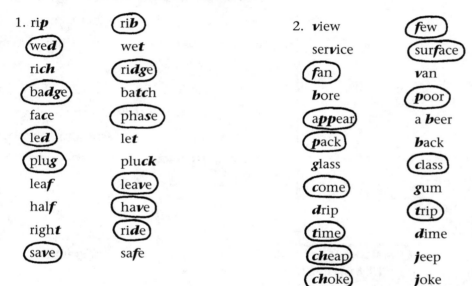

1. rip   (rib)
   (wed)   wet
   rich   (ridge)
   (badge)   batch
   face   (phase)
   (led)   let
   (plug)   pluck
   leaf   (leave)
   half   (have)
   right   (ride)
   (save)   safe

2. view   (few)
   service   (surface)
   (fan)   van
   bore   (poor)
   (appear)   a beer
   (pack)   back
   glass   (class)
   (come)   gum
   drip   (trip)
   (time)   dime
   (cheap)   jeep
   (choke)   joke

Consonant One: /θ/as in *think*

LISTENING ACTIVITY 2

a. B	d. M	g. B	j. E
b. B	e. E	h. B	k. M
c. E	f. M	i. E	l. E

LISTENING ACTIVITY 3

a. 1	d. 1	g. 2	i. 2
b. 1	e. 2	h. 1	j. 1
c. 2	f. 1		

LISTENING ACTIVITY 4   a. __X__ It's not thick.

b. __X__ She wants to play baseball.

c. __X__ It's not a bush.

d. __X__ I'm almost certain she's two now.

e. __X__ He can't solve the problem alone.

LISTENING ACTIVITY 5

What Makes You Thin?

What makes you ***thin***? Most people ***think*** that dieting is the answer, but researchers say that exercise is the best way to be ***thin.*** In one study, ***thirty-two*** men who were sedentary were put on an exercise program. They walked, jogged, and ran ***throughout*** the one-year program. The first ***thing*** the study showed was that the men who had exercised the most lost the most weight. The second ***thing*** the study revealed was that the men who lost the most weight ate more too. The researchers ***theorize*** that fat people don't really eat a lot. Their problem is that they are inactive.

COMMUNICATIVE PRACTICE 2:

Most

1. Computer Programmer
2. Airplane Pilot
3. Surgeon
4. Book Author
5. Mathematician
6. College Professor
7. Auto Painter
8. Bank Teller
9. Dairy Farmer

Least   10. Construction Worker*

*Source: Les Kranz. *Jobs Rated Almanac.* New York: Pharos Books, Scripps-Howard Company, 1988, pp. 223–225.

Consonant Two: /f/ as in *fine*

LISTENING ACTIVITY 2

a. B	d. E	g. M	j. E
b. E	e. E	h. B	k. B
c. B	f. M	i. B	l. E

LISTENING ACTIVITY 3

a. 1	d. 2	g. 2	j. 2
b. 1	e. 2	h. 2	k. 1
c. 2	f. 1	i. 1	l. 1

LISTENING ACTIVITY 4

a. __X__ That's why the coffee tastes so good.

b. __X__ Do you have proof?

c. __X__ We never get raises.

d. __X__ Did you see her go by?

e. __X__ In the small appliances department.

LISTENING ACTIVITY 5

VideoPhones

In 1992, AT&T began *offering* customers a Video*Phone,* a *telephone* with a small color screen that allows callers to look at each other while they are talking. *If* callers, however, *prefer* to be invisible, there is a special *feature* that will close the lens of the camera. Now, in addition to popular *phones* for your cars and video *telephone conferencing* systems that have become almost standard in the *offices* of big businesses, you can plug Video*Phones* into standard *telephone* outlets in your home.

Consonant Three: /ʃ/ as in *she*

LISTENING ACTIVITY 2

a. B	d. E	g. M	i. M
b. B	e. M	h. E	j. M
c. E	f. E		

LISTENING ACTIVITY 3

a. 1	d. 1	g. 1	i. 2
b. 1	e. 2	h. 2	j. 2
c. 2	f. 1		

LISTENING ACTIVITY 4

a. __X__ His sheets.

b. __X__ Should I put it in the refrigerator?

c. __X__ Sure. I used to play baseball.

d. __X__ She's in complete agreement.

LISTENING ACTIVITY 5

Shyness

About 92 million Americans are *shy.* Researchers are taking an interest in *shyness* and have reached a number of different conclusions. According to one study, *social relations* these days are more complex, and *shyness* is becoming a *national* concern. Another study found that only about half of the *shy* people were tense or *anxious* in *social situations,* contrary to popular belief. And still another found that *shy* people tend to be more stable in their *relationships.* Some psychologists think that *shyness* may be inherited, while others think that *shyness* is cultural.

Consonant Four: /r/ as in *right*

LISTENING ACTIVITY 2

a. B	d. E	g. M	j. M
b. B	e. M	h. M	k. M
c. E	f. B	i. E	l. B

LISTENING ACTIVITY 3

a. 1	e. 1	i. 2	l. 2
b. 1	f. 1	j. 2	m. 2
c. 2	g. 2	k. 1	n. 1
d. 1	h. 1		

LISTENING ACTIVITY 4

a. __X__ You need the short one.

b. __X__ At church.

c. __X__ In the sky.

d. __X__ He's holding a ball.

e. __X__ The leaves are killing the grass.

f. __X__ I like the southwest.

LISTENING ACTIVITY 5

Butterflies in Your Stomach

If you've ever given a **report** in **front** of a class or a **group** of people, you know the feeling. Your **heart races,** your blood **pressure rises,** your hands **start** to shake, your **throat** gets **dry,** and you get **butter**flies in your stomach. What causes your body to **react** this way? When you're **nervous** or **frightened,** your glands **release** adrenalin into your blood**stream.** The **adrenalin** causes your muscles to tense up. It also causes **increased** motion in your stomach muscles. As a **result,** your stomach **produces more** acid than it needs for digestion. The acid feels like **butter**flies in your stomach.

Consonant Five: /v/ as in *vote*

LISTENING ACTIVITY 2

a. B	d. E	g. M	i. E
b. B	e. B	h. B	j. M
c. M	f. M		

LISTENING ACTIVITY 3

a. 1	e. 2	i. 1	l. 2
b. 1	f. 1	j. 2	m. 1
c. 2	g. 1	k. 2	n. 1
d. 1	h. 1		

LISTENING ACTIVITY 4

a. __X__ On the bike.

b. __X__ A dry, red wine.

c. __X__ They remind me of her.

d. __X__ The engine died.

e. __X__ He loves to ride waves.

LISTENING ACTIVITY 5

Valentine's Day

For **over** 100 years, it has been popular to **give** cards, flowers, gifts, and other tokens of **love** on February 14, St. **Valentine's** Day in the United States. There are **several** explanations for the origin of this holiday; **however,** the most **believable** is that St. **Valentine's** Day is a **survival** of a February 15th Roman **festival.** During this **festival,** bachelors picked names of women to **discover** who their **"valentines"** or **lovers** would be for the coming year. The couples then exchanged gifts and sometimes **even** became engaged.

Answer Key for Appendix C

1. Vowel 2: /ɪ/ as in *hit*

LISTENING ACTIVITY 3

a. 1	d. 2	g. 2	i. 1
b. 1	e. 2	h. 1	j. 2
c. 2	f. 1		

LISTENING ACTIVITY 4

a. __X__ Yes, on the ice.

b. __X__ It was a good crop.

c. __X__ Yes. She's packing her bags now.

d. __X__ Yes, with the hammer.

e. __X__ In the medicine chest.

LISTENING ACTIVITY 5

Drinking and Health Risks

People often ***lift*** a glass to toast good health. ***Drinking*** may indeed lower the ***risk*** of several diseases, according to some ***interesting statistics*** released by the Harvard School of Public Health. Researchers found that up to one to two ***drinks*** each day ***diminished*** the ***risk*** of heart attack, stroke, and fatal heart disease by about ***twenty-six*** percent in men and up to ***fifty*** percent in ***women.*** One researcher warned, however, that ***women*** with a family ***history*** of breast cancer should ***limit drinking*** since alcohol is ***linked*** to a higher ***risk*** of breast cancer.

2. Vowel 4: /ε/ as in *met*

LISTENING ACTIVITY 3

a. 2	d. 1	g. 1	i. 1
b. 2	e. 2	h. 2	j. 1
c. 1	f. 1		

LISTENING ACTIVITY 4

a. __X__ For dinner tonight.

b. __X__ I'm sorry you missed him.

c. __X__ It was too spicy.

d. __X__ Did you like him?

e. __X__ Nice and sharp.

LISTENING ACTIVITY 5

Airbags

The airbag has become standard equipment in new cars. It is stored in the ***center*** of the steering wheel, and, in an accident, quickly inflates to ***help*** save a driver's life. The airbag has electronic ***sensors*** that can feel a crash as it begins to happen. The ***sensors set*** off a small can of nitrogen gas, which rushes into the bag. The soft bag ***protects*** the driver and ***then*** it deflates. Airbags are only useful in ***head***-on or rear-***end*** accidents. During a side collision, a driver needs a seat***belt*** for ***protection.***

3. Vowel 7: /ʌ/ as in *nut*

LISTENING ACTIVITY 3

a. 2   d. 1   g. 1   i. 2

b. 2   e. 1   h. 1   j. 1

c. 1   f. 2

LISTENING ACTIVITY 4

a. __X__ Yes. It has fur.

b. __X__ For coffee.

c. __X__ I hate that shade of green.

d. __X__ I can't untie it.

e. __X__ No. I lost.

LISTENING ACTIVITY 5

Foreign Student Numbers Are Up

During the 1990-91 academic year, foreign students ***studying*** in U.S. colleges and universities ***jumped*** to an all-time high of *407,500*. This ***number*** represents an increase of 5.3% over the previous year. Asian students accounted for 40% of the total and ***much*** of the growth. In fact, Japanese student enrollment ***doubled*** in the previous three academic years. Substantial increases were noted from Europe as well. The ***number*** of students ***coming*** from Eastern European ***countries*** was ***up*** 42% over the previous year.

COMMUNICATIVE PRACTICE 2:

1. LONG UNDERWEAR   (**lo**ng = /ɑ/; ***u***nderwear = /ʌ/)

2. SANDBOX   (sandb**o**x = /ɑ/)

3. CIRCLES UNDER THE EYES   (***u***nder = /ʌ/)

4. TOUCHDOWN   (t**ou**chdown = /ʌ/)

5. SIX FEET UNDERGROUND   (***u***nderground = /ʌ/)

6. NEON LIGHTS   (ne**o**n = /ɑ/)

7. DOUBLE TROUBLE   (d**ou**ble and tr**ou**ble = /ʌ/)

4. Vowel 10: /ʊ/ as in *took*

LISTENING ACTIVITY 3   a. 1   c. 2   e. 2   g. 1

b. 2   d. 1   f. 1   h. 2

LISTENING ACTIVITY 4   a. __X__ It's all over the fireplace.

b. __X__ He'll have to swim somewhere else.

c. __X__ It has to cool.

d. __X__ To the cleaners.

LISTENING ACTIVITY 5

Eating Out

People in the United States are spending less time ***cooking*** and more time eating out in restaurants. In fact, many people in the United States eat out on the average of four times a week. If you invite someone to join you for dinner in a restaurant, here are some general guidelines. You ***should*** phone first in order to find out if you need a reservation. When you invite someone to dinner, you ***should*** be prepared to pay the bill. However, sometimes the guests ***would*** rather pay so that they won't feel indebted to you. When the bill arrives, ***look*** to see if the tip has been added to the cost of the food. Most restaurants do not add the tip to the bill. You ***should*** leave a tip equal to 15% of the bill if the service was adequate. If the restaurant is expensive or if the service was especially ***good,*** you ***could*** leave up to 20% of the bill.

5. Vowel 8: /ɑ / as in *not*

LISTENING ACTIVITY 3

a. 1   d. 2   g. 2   i. 1

b. 1   e. 1   h. 2   j. 2

c. 1   f. 1

LISTENING ACTIVITY 4

a. __X__ From the accident.

b. __X__ He'll be excited.

c. __X__ Yes. I mailed them.

d. __X__ No. The market's out of fish.

LISTENING ACTIVITY 5

Jobs and Hormones

Testosterone, the hormone ***responsible*** for sex drive and aggression, may have some influence on our choice of ***jobs.*** According to a recent study by a Georgia State University ***psychology*** professor, people with high levels of testosterone ***opt*** for professions in which they face severe competition in order to succeed. Actors have the most testosterone of all; ***doctors*** and trial lawyers rank high also. The lowest levels of testosterone are found among nurses and ministers who devote themselves to comforting, not competing with, others. Since women have lower levels of testosterone than men in general, the researcher ***cautions*** that success is ***not*** dependent on hormones. ***Biology*** is important, but it is ***not*** destiny.

Note: In some dialects of American English, the au in c*au*tious is /ɔ/; in others, it is /ɑ /.